PLENARY INDULGENCES

by

Michael P. Riccards

The cover picture is from Domenico di Michelino's painting of Dante Aligheiri in Purgatory, Florence, 1465.

The poem, "And God Said No," on page 23 was written by Claudia Minden Weisz.

The picture on page 87 was drawn by Robert Quinn.

ISBN:13: 978-1548137779

DEDICATION

To the people of Somalia,

South Sudan, and Yemen

that they may soon know peace and prosperity

CONTENTS

PREFACE

In a previous book I have compiled about 60 short vignettes featuring my grandfather. Raffaele Finelli is the protagonist through which we view the simple complexities of life. He was born in southern Italy, came to America at 16, and spent most of his life as a gardener who especially loved the beauty and bounty of nature. Some libraries have catalogued this book as a biography, and others as creative fiction. Perhaps they are both right.

The responses I received to *Brief Encounters* has been especially positive, and I thank the readers for their kindness. But I think people were really less enthralled by my technical virtuosity, than they were with the personality of the hero. Grandpa was a traditional man, wedded to traditional values, who tried to keep those virtues alive as he moved from a very old culture to a new one of great movement and achievement.

He comes across in *Brief Encounters* as a decent, loyal, honorable man who served the needs of people less fortunate than his family. At his funeral, an old African-American woman rose up in the middle of the ceremony in the Catholic church in Madison, N.J., and proclaimed, "he was a prince of a man." Apparently for years he had provided the elderly widow with food and even flowers. May we all end up with such praise.

Grandpa lived in an America increasingly full of con men, hucksters, hedge fund managers, and politicians who insist that they operate above the constraints of truth.

We are even more bedeviled by that world today. My collection, done with Cheryl A. Flagg, was meant to show an alternative to that new amoral world. Readers again and again have commented on Grandpa's integrity, as if we had lost virtue in our own time. I think we have, and Grandpa shows unselfconsciously an alternative world of morality, one more satisfying than the simple chasing of a buck and one-upmanship.

I will let that book stand on its own feet, as Grandpa stood on his. It seemed to me though that there was a larger universe of experiences that one could investigate. And so for nearly thirty more vignettes and four plays, I have tried to focus on more contemporary moral dilemmas.

When I was a child in post-World War II America, scientists were exploring the new worlds of something called DNA, the physical building blocks of life. What has been extraordinary is how many of our questions on life and reproduction have been answered, but in this second volume, *Plenary Indulgences*, I have tried to look at our emotional DNA, the strands and components of our ethical and spiritual lives. That DNA is even more complicated, for there are nuances that twist and change and finally give us our unique personality, character, or psyche.

Carl Jung and Joseph Campbell have postulated that we inherit from our ancestors stereotypical ways of thinking, fearing, and worshipping that stamp our species. I think Freud is more correct, We work out in our conscious and dream states of mind mixes of psychology, philosophy, and even medical prescriptions that make us unique in both our neuroses and in our ways of coming to deal with the challenges of the brief time that we live in.

Most of us exist on the surfaces of that reality, but there are a few individuals who are seeking to understand greater realities through prayer, contemplation, and meditation. I frequently get the question, "How can a guy with a Ph.D. believe in such traditional nonsense?" When we are dead, we are dead. Like last spring's flowers, we rot after we bloom. Yet I have been infatuated by those who dedicate their lives to faith, mystery, and a vague sense of transcendence.

For that reason and perhaps because of a sense of vanity, I have printed four of my verse plays on Catholic saints. It is not that other ways of life in the world do not have equally holy people; it is just that this is the tradition in which I have been raised and which makes it most easy for me to put into verse. If you wish to see other sorts of saintly individuals from different cultures come alive, examine the fine work of Karen Armstrong, a one-time nun and now an uncertain agnostic-atheist of great sensitivity to all major traditions.

St. Patrick, the supreme patron of Ireland, fought his major battles against both Druid priests and British Catholic bishops. At the presentation of this play the first time in New Jersey, the audience spontaneously rose in the end to sing "Hail Saint Patrick" in traditional Gaelic. They put the ending on my play, and I was proud of their participation.

The second play is the story of the increasingly popular St. Francis of Assisi. Born to wealth, he became the patron saint of everything from the humane treatment of animals to the environment. To him, God subsumed nature, and since he so loved God, he loved all His manifestations. He died an early, painful death.

His female counterpart was St. Clare of Assisi, who was often at odds with her own Church in trying to form the Poor Ladies, committed not to the easy paths of living, but to extensive fasting, prayer, chastity, and deep concern for her fellow human beings. Incredibly by 2011 there were over 20,000 women living this austere life in communities in over 75 countries.

And the last dramatic figure in this book is that of a once little-known Polish mystic, Sister Faustina. She also died too young, in her early thirties, but in a few years she gave to the world a new devotional way of life based in large part on her diary which I have sought to dramatize. In it she emphasizes the importance of mercy, not justice or old-fashioned retribution. The name and devotions of Divine Mercy have begun to become a worldwide phenomenon, especially since her canonization by St. John Paul II in 2001.

These four people represent a different level of consciousness, one that few of us will ever achieve, but there are still many Eastern mystics who embrace something similar. I enclose these plays because of their similarity and because in seeking to understand our essential DNA, we will have to come to grips with this old sensibility as we have come to grips with the day-to-day activities that have been outlined in the "Parables" part.

THE PARABLES

1. TWO TON TONY

To: Dad who was there

Every town or neighborhood has a hero who is highly regarded by the citizenry, especially children. Some heroes are local figures, but others become well known outside the boundaries of the region or even the nation. Orange, New Jersey, was a modest-sized, working class suburb of New York City, and had become a locus for Italian-American and black families.

The Great Depression was a terrible time for people to get through, and some families even lacked food to feed their families. Suicides increased, men were unemployed, women took in piecework from nearby factories, and children gave up their youth to whatever activity they could to join in paying the bills. In one family in Orange, the members had Easter soup that was made of ketchup, spices, and water. The boys undertook vast deliveries of newspapers, especially in the elegant Llewellyn Park area where Thomas Alva Edison and Harry Firestone lived. The hardworking mother of that collection of poor children desperately wanted all of her children to go to college, for she believed that education was the key to the American dream. With meager funds she pushed all her children, even her two girls, which is rare in Italian-American families, to go to college.

There wasn't much entertainment in the house, except the rudimentary radio where the kids could hear baseball and boxing, then the two great American pastimes.

The blacks had no heroes in baseball at that time, but were deeply committed to the great heavyweight boxer, Joe Louis, the Brown Bomber. The Italians, of course, had in baseball a legion of heroes, the most famous being Joe DiMaggio, but Orange had its own local boxer as well, the rotund, crude, foul-talking barkeeper, Tony Galento, who was 5'8" and weighed in at 240 pounds.

Galento would fight anyone, anytime, for anything. One night he beat three competitors in a row, and drank beer between the fights. But in the depths of the Depression, he was seen as a possible contender against Joe Louis. Louis fought a string of second-level fighters whom he inelegantly called "the bum of the month club."

Galento operated a bar called "The Nut Club," right on Day Street, not too far from the house in which a young college boy lived with five siblings. He came to admire Galento, and showed up at the bar, not so much to drink, for he had little spare change, but mainly to talk to Tony about his strange career.

Galento was frank, "Look Ponzione, they call me a dirty fighter. I am smaller than they are, with a short reach. I gotta make every shot count. I do that by lowering my body and hitting them in the stomach or kidneys. Christ, is that effective."

Ponzione responded, "Is that why they call you Two Ton Tony?"

Galento laughed, "Shit. That came from the fact that once I missed practice and told the manager that I was late because I had to deliver two tons of ice to the housewives for their iceboxes. But the Two Ton label stuck and it scared the crazy niggers in Newark."

Like all Italian Americans, Ponzione was enthusiastic, having one of their own as the world champion. "Do you think you will get a shot at the title?"

"I don't know. Those damn Jews are taking forever to book me. They created this Joe Louis as a national legend. After Jack Johnson they wanted a clean *moulinyan*, one who wasn't so arrogant and who didn't screw white girls. Louis screws white girls, yet he keeps it low key. But his wife knows. At least I am pure."

"Louis had affairs with Sonia Henie and Mae West. We have all heard about it at the barbershop."

"Hell, everyone has done Mae West. I saw your old man last night coming home at 2 a.m. from the Italian-American Club. When does he work? My wife and your mother go to the 6 a.m. Mass together at the Capuchin church down the hill. They are both religious women. I think they make up for their men. God decreed it that way. Why the hell are you going to college? Who has the type of money to do that anyhow?"

Ponzione responded, "It is my mother's dream. She wants us to be true Americans."

Tony thought a while and then countered, "How the hell can you be an American with a name like Ponzione? I don't even know how to translate that myself."

Ponzione quietly replied, "I changed it in college to Charlie and then to Patrick. I will change the last name after the war if it comes."

"I intend to use Two Ton Tony forever. It will be on my tombstone at St. Joseph's over there."

And then he dropped his rough voice, "And I could beatta that bum, that black palooka. I watch films on how that German Schmeling knocked him around in that first fight. Louis has a tendency to drop his right hand, and then step back. Pat, Charlie, Ponzione, or whatever you are called, I will charge him like a mad bull, and when he leaves an opening pound him with a right. My trainers don't want me to crouch over, but stand tall and fight him. Stand tall at 5'8"? What the hell I am supposed to look like? A fat Jim Broderick?"

Ponzione just listened to Galento as he plotted out his strategy like Julius Caesar coming into Gaul. "Last month, I bet a guy $10 after I ate 50 hot dogs, and won the fight. I used the winnings to buy beer for everybody!"

But the *Newark Star Ledger* sports writers and the *National Sporting News* complained that Louis, the great champion, neglected to fight people like Galento. "The Great White Hope," they called him.

Finally in July 1939, Galento drove himself to Yankee Stadium. Louis, dressed in a $100 cashmere coat, arrived with his completely black entourage. Tony came alone from Orange to the stadium. The night before the fight, he and the kid walked down Day Street. Tony was usually a loud blowhard, but he was very quiet that night. Some said he was really afraid of Louis, but Galento said he was afraid of no one. He'd beat the *moulinyan* bum. Before the fight, he'd called Louis at his training camp in Pompton Plains, New Jersey, and harassed him over the phone again and again.

Louis was favored 6 to 1, but a good portion of the crowd cheered for the white, working man. In the first round, Galento with a quick jab knocked the jaw of the immortal Louis. Then in the second round the expert champion craftsman took Galento's face apart with short jabs. In the third it was a draw, but Louis was clearly ahead. Then in the fourth round, Galento jumped out of his corner, surprised Louis, and the champion celebrity dropped his right glove and raised his left glove up a little. He eventually created an opening and Tony pushed all of his considerable power at Louis's chin. He hit him so hard that Louis was knocked to the canvas and fell back on his head. The crowd went still. Except for Max Schmeling in their first bout, nobody had ever hit Louis like that. No one had ever knocked him to the canvas. Galento for several seconds stood over the famed champion, watching Louis below him. How long it lasted no one knows. Perhaps seconds, perhaps minutes, perhaps a glorious eternity to Tony. He would forever be known as the man who floored the immortal Louis. But by the eighth round, Tony was wearing down. The better-shaped and disciplined Louis went into high gear. Arthur Donovan, the legendary referee, called the match for the current heavyweight champion of the world, Joe Louis. Galento was cut to pieces, heavily stitched up by Doc Stern, and sent to Orange Memorial Hospital. Later he went by himself back to the streets of Orange. The next night he stood up in the tavern. Waiting for him was Ponzione. Galento humbly responded, "Did I let you and the guys down, kid?"

"Oh, no. You were magnificent. We all were so proud of you. You will forever be remembered as the man who knocked down Louis. It was incredible."

Tony smiled through his bandages. "Yeah, I was good, wasn't I? Boy, Louis looked scared. Have you seen the pictures? Take a look at today's *Newark Star Ledger*. If my manager had let me fight the way I wanted to, I would have knocked him out totally. And if the Jews had put more money behind me to train at Madame Bey on River Road in Chatham, I'd be the champion forever."

"I'd bet you would Tony. We were all so proud of you."

"I will tell you when we were alone the night before, I was a little quiet and rather scared, I will admit. Ah, it was only that I wanted to be a contender. I wanted to be the champion."

Years later Tony boxed a kangaroo and a 560-pound bear (the bear beat him). He wrestled with an octopus and became more of an attraction than a champion. He ended up doing a cameo role in *On the Waterfront* with Marlon

Brando. He lost two legs to diabetes and died from it. He was 79. Ponzione lived a peaceful life with a respectable white-collared job and a fine family. He died of painful stomach cancer at 73. And Joe Louis was cited by the federal government for income tax evasion. Louis went on cocaine, and ended up in a mental institution for a while like his father, screaming the FBI or the Mafia was after him. He went back to fighting again to pay his bills, and lost to an Italian-American boxer named Rocky Marciano from Brockton, Massachusetts, in the eighth round. Marciano ended up dying at 46 in an airplane crash; Louis died at 68. These lives intertwined, if only for a short period of time.

As the famed balladeer Johnny Cash has written about the cycles of life,

> There's man goin' 'round takin' names.
> And he decides who to free and who to blame,
> Everyone won't be treated all the same.
> There'll be a golden ladder reachin' down
> When the man comes 'round…
>
> Whoever is unjust let him be unjust still.
> Whoever is righteous, let him be righteous still.
> Whoever is filthy, let him be filthy still.
> Listen to the words long written down,
> When the man comes 'round.

.
.

2. SUPERMAN

On a modest farm in Kansas, there grew up a tall, gangly boy, Aaron Samson, who loved to figure out how machines worked. That made him a very remarkable asset to the county, and his high school counselor and principal recommended him for a full scholarship to Massachusetts Institute of Technology in Cambridge, farther east than anyone in the family had ever gone. He deferentially applied and to the surprise of everyone he was accepted on full scholarship. Unlike many students there, he was interested in classical physics, which meant Isaac Newton. And as he studied Newton's *Principia*, he moved on to Newton's correspondence and to his notebooks. To his total surprise, he found that the great man of science believed in alchemy, the turning of base metals into gold, and he was sympathetic to the medieval black arts in general. One of his most interesting and least known notes was a complex calculus to figure out how long one would live. Within a day's term Newton could predict a person's death, and in fact did it for himself.

Aaron used that strategic methodology first to turn some steel pellets into gold and was suddenly financially emancipated. And then he dared to calculate the day of his own death. He wondered though, did anyone really want to know that? Death came when he predicted it, not like the thief in the night. Did he really want to live with the sword of Damocles over his head? But that power certainly got the best of him, and he found out that one good side effect of the strange workings was that he now feared nothing before his final date. For a good length of time he was immune from disease, violence, or even serious accident. And one evening he realized that the world around him was full of bad people doing bad things. Maybe he could put a stop to some of that.

He then took a black t-shirt and painted a big "S" on it for his last name, wore a pair of dark sneakers, and he couldn't be recognized because he wore a black mask. No one should know that he had explored that deeply into nature. He threw his new gear in the back of his car and was riding to an antique bookstore, looking for more of Newton's work. But on the way down Morrissey Boulevard, he saw a driver hit a telephone pole and flip over. Aaron suddenly stopped his car and saw the man was trapped. He ran into the offices of the

Boston Globe and screamed for help, and a group of men rushed to try to turn over the vehicle, but it was just too heavy. The driver was trapped into his own death. Aaron opened up his own car's back door, put on the outfit that he had created, emerged taller, and screamed to the Dorchester neighborhood for more help. Out of the triple-deckers poured large muscular Irish boys, tumbling into the streets and helping to turn the car back over. Remarkably the driver was all right. The heroes all looked around for their leader, but the man with the "S" was gone, and only Aaron stood nearby. It turns out that the driver was a reporter for the *Boston Globe,* Jimmy Olsen, who had too much to drink at an office party. He would write the story of his escape, and the next day he got a byline for the first time in the *Boston Globe*, "Super Man Rescues Reporter, Dorchester Residents Save Olsen."

That story was the first time the WASP-owned *Boston Globe* had said anything nice about their Irish neighbors, so the residents chalked it up to the remarkable masked man. Then two nights later a black woman in Roxbury was hurrying to the pharmacy to buy medication for her very sick boy. With all her savings in a paisley bag, she hoped it was enough. Then between the buildings a young thug moved out to grab her pocketbook which she held on to for dear life, but he was young and strong, and she was fighting a losing battle, especially when he pulled out a switchblade and aimed it at her wrist. But then a masked man wearing an "S" shirt hit the assailant over the head with a 2 x 4, and he just collapsed.

Superman indeed headed over to the pharmacy with her, walked her home, and two days later the *Globe* featured an interview with a proud black woman and her happy child, saying "Super Man Strikes Again, Saves Sick Baby." The mom said, "He was like an angel of God come to protect me. Thank God for our Super Man."

A week later a female worker was walking sprightly through the dark Boston Common and out jumped a huge man determined to rape the young stylish woman. She screamed and screamed as he persisted, and then the desperate man felt a noose tied around his neck with one gigantic pull against his windpipe. The rapist decided he would prefer to keep his life more than satisfy his penis and he ran away. The young lady claimed protection was provided by somebody wearing an "S" on his t-shirt. Jimmy Olsen interviewed her and helped her provide details on Super Man, "He is the protector of women in this awful city," she exclaimed, or so Jimmy wrote.

A month later, the adventures of Super Man stopped a lynching in far-away Mississippi by tossing a fiery torchlight at some good ole boys and freeing up a black man tied to a tree. He called Super Man "the new Lincoln." And so Olsen wrote this story as well. And now he had his own column.

Then in New York City, Super Man appeared in the Bronx and ended a drug gang fight, simply by raising his hands. All the druggies vanished and the *New York Post* claimed to have found a dozen sources for the story.

Meanwhile in the Midwest a poor family was desperately trying to remove its tractor out of a mudbank and claimed that Super Man by his bare hands was the person who helped pull it out.

Super Man seemed to be everywhere and in such rapid succession that his appearances would only be possible if he could fly from one place to another. This was especially incredible since the next day he helped the Salvation Army provide food to flood victims in New Orleans. They dedicated the Mardi Gras parade to Super Man, and presented a huge floral arrangement at the base of the statue of the heroic Andrew Jackson. Olsen reported that bad guys in that city sought to end his life, but their bullets popped off him. Cars aimed at his form but just stopped dead in the street. More and more the forces of evil were on the run. Jimmy Olsen finally interviewed Super Man, and quoted him as saying that he was committed to "truth, justice and the American way," and people loved the slogan. As the years passed by, DC Comics hired Jerry Siegel to write a Superman comic book full of his adventures and tales. It quickly became a best seller, and there were Superman costumes everywhere, and people sworn to fight for good.

As Aaron got older, he realized the days of his demise were coming. The day before his death he burned all his Superman regalia for he wanted only the legend to go to his grave. On his night stand he had only two items: Newton's *Principia* and Siegel's *The Adventures of Superman.*

3. WELCOME SINNERS

The Greeks say that a man is driven by his character, a word that derives itself from "written in the soul." We are so much creatures of habit that our random thoughts are captives of those predispositions. Such was the case with Allen Hurt who was raised in a conventional middle-class background of moderate Catholic views and temperate virtues. One summer young Allen had decided to go with his family on a car trip from Madison, New Jersey to the beautiful cathedral of Saint Anne de Beaupre in Montreal. It was a long, arduous trip in the 1954 black and blue Plymouth, up the New York highways and across the Quebec roads. One day he and his family went over the Queen Victoria Bridge, a wood structure that looked like it was older than the beloved monarch herself.

Allen lived in a quiet world of his own, and this was the first excursion that he had made outside of the borders of that world. According to Catholic tradition, Saint Anne was the mother of the Virgin Mary, Jesus' grandmother, and the shrine became a great center of popular healing. In fact, the French Canadians built a modest wooden structure that was painted in dark gray and laid on the side of a mountain near the St. Lawrence River. In the chapel were endless signs of miracles performed—crutches and canes, wheelchairs, harnesses, belts on metal plates—all the paraphernalia that was then so characteristic of nineteenth century medicine. Each of these items represented a cure, and the participants went home, free at last of afflictions and hopelessness.

Over the years, thousands went to the new cathedral and arrived near Saint Anne's feast day of July 26. They were the disabled, the maimed, the wounded, the slow-witted, the unfortunates from all over the world. They marched down the main street, eight abreast, as best they could on the first day of prayers for a cure from the saint. They went up the stairs slowly into the basilica, prayed before the oak carved statue of the great mother and then left. Over the years enough claimed cures were verified that the appeal of the devotion grew into a world-wide cult. The year that Allen went witnessed a deaf man from Orange, New Jersey, who came to pray for his very sick wife. She was not cured, but his deafness went away, and the entire Italian-American neighborhood in that town crowded into the Capuchin church, Our Lady of Mount Carmel, to give thanks.

Allen's family stood for hours and watched the parade of the handicapped and at the end he felt nauseous. His father said he also was upset about all those people, and he bought the two of them a glass of orange juice to settle their stomachs. His mother, a former nurse, did not have that reaction.

For years after, in school and in college, Allen avoided socializing with handicapped kids. They made him feel uncomfortable. He had little sympathy for special needs education, endless ramps, special accommodations, reserved parking spaces. Allen argued, "If people are that crippled, they should just stay home and watch life on TV." When the country talked of people being mentally challenged, he insisted on still calling them "retards." He would not make any compromises within his character.

Then at the height of his powers, at the age of 53, he suffered a massive heart attack and ended up in the hospital for bypass surgery. After an unusually long convalescence, due in part to a post-operative infection, he had to use crutches and wheelchairs and pull himself up by a bar across his bed. At times he could barely get up and was endlessly frustrated by nurses who never seemed to answer his night calls.

One day he insisted on taking a shower, but since he could not stand up, the unsympathetic nurse on duty just put him in the wheelchair, took him into an aluminum box and gave him a washcloth and soap, and turned on a hose. She washed him down like a dirty animal in the mud of a river.

For some weeks after that, Allen saw more than his share of suffering and of the quick loss of faculties. He observed that many patients characterized as having dementia were just stupefied by the monotonous days, the pictureless walls, and the lack of any true intellectual conversation.

One afternoon an elderly patient talked to him about how to outgrow the Dow Jones industrial average, and he plotted carefully his daily guesses in the stock pages. If he had been in a more robust environment he would have been extremely rich. Another elderly woman told him truthfully she had been a Rockette at Radio City Music Hall.

After some weeks, Allen refused to stay and went home where he practiced physical therapy for the most basic tasks. The most difficult part of the regime was climbing stairs; the most telling part of his surgery was a long ugly scar from his throat down to his chest. Every morning he recognized what he had gone through.

One afternoon he watched out of the bay window in his office and saw a handicapped boy pulling himself out of a wheelchair into the front seat of his mother's car. Allen looked around the room and said to no one in particular, "You don't know how hard that is unless you have to do it." And he realized that he had grown a touch of genuine empathy.

A week later he was driving past the Catholic church that served the medical staff of the hospital area across the street. It was called St. Camillus after the health care patron in France. There this man, an old Hispanic, was trying to lay a long cement path on the side with iron bars for people to use. The front of St. Camillus was set on six difficult steps and the pastor was attempting to deal with the problems of the handicapped. For some reason Allen stopped his car and watched the old man having problems in laying the cement, placing the iron bars and calculating the exact altitude of the ramp at the same time. He got out of the car, walked over and said casually, "Need some help on this?" The old man quietly nodded, and together the two of them put the ramp down and stretched across the yellow tape to stop traffic from using the side entrance until the cement dried. When the work was done, the entrance had a sign that said, "Sinners Welcome." When the laborer left the job, the old man wanted to share his fee with Allen, but he just responded, "No, it's for a good cause." Whenever he saw the laborer's work, he stared at the ramp and realized how important it was. But cement doesn't wash away after it dries, and so the Arrow shirt and tie that he wore that day became history.

Always when he went to the church he went up the ramp, not the stairs, and he looked at the sign above him. He became proud of his part in making the ramp, and humble for there are many types of sin that only the one who commits them knows.

4. BETTER LIVING THROUGH CHEMISTRY

Man has been given domain over all nature, and yet he is a part of nature. He is driven to control the environment around him, but also within himself. One young student, Philip Dryden, loved the mastery of nature and was drawn especially to chemistry as an intense way of controlling his and others' lives. He was a ruggedly built boy with broad shoulders, strong torso, and lightning quick reflexes. In school he gravitated to baseball, and ended up on a partial scholarship at the University of Southern California.

He was a superb second baseman, and hit .406 for the university team. His coach wanted him to try out for the Los Angeles Dodgers, but he was more academically oriented than one would have imagined. Like a lot of well-built athletes, he met through a friend a beautiful young girl finishing up her degree in fashion design at UCLA. She was tall, stately even at twenty, had blonde hair, sparkling blue eyes, and long legs.

They were incredibly attracted to each other. She was passionately in love with him even with all his shortcomings and his fixation on chemistry. Whether he was in love with her is unclear, for to be honest he did not know what love was. He knew it meant a strong attraction, but he also realized that with her it was powerfully sexual, for she was breathtakingly beautiful.

One afternoon as they made love in his room, he was propping himself on his elbows looking at her face. Her eyes were dreamily closed, and she looked like a portrait of a young Marilyn Monroe that he had seen in *Gentlemen Prefer Blondes*. Her body was tight, toned, and anxious to have him in her. Her only flaw, if one could call it that, was that she was rather flat-chested.

He was not sure if he was in love after all the afternoons and evenings they spent together in their senior year. Would he sacrifice himself for her? Is that love? Would he stop being attracted to other women on campus? Was that exclusiveness love or could one have love for more than one person in the same way? Was love more than the right chemical mix, heightened by smells? He honestly didn't know love, but he was attracted to her, and so they did the conventional thing and married.

He got himself a high-paying job at Dow Chemical Company, reflecting his strong academic record. Phil really believed in their slogan, "Better Living through Chemistry." When his wife was somewhat critical of the chemical world, he cited to her how they had destroyed malaria in Africa, nearly conquered AIDS and Ebola, and made a real dent in infant mortality.

Man was mastering nature, he said, and all benefitted from its dominance. The two of them became for Dow executives a true power couple and were sent together up and down California to plead the case for a beautiful chemical future.

Phil kept up his personal research and wrote down his experiments. All were well-thought out and seemed to be successful. But something always went wrong. He was the master of nature, but in the end, nature got new strengths, new guile, and avoided his hypotheses and his final findings.

Phil loved the lecture circuit and was proud to have his lovely wife by his side. She seemed so sweet and generous, so perfect, and people were drawn to her unassuming beauty.

But still he became fixated on her figure; she was so attractive except for that flat chest, the almost mannequin figure that showed off her clothes better than her figure. He tried to say nothing to her, for she loved him so. But finally, he took her aside after one social function. "You look so beautiful tonight as usual, but you could look remarkably better if you had a more shapely figure."

"Shapely, how honey?"

"If you only had breasts that matched the beauty of your face and hips, you'd be a goddess."

She became immediately quiet and self-conscious. She thought to herself, *All these years he has been ashamed of me in front of his associates and friends. Did she hurt him at work, keep him back while everybody was looking at him since he was so handsome, and she was so deficient?* She stopped going to joint engagements with him, not to punish him but out of embarrassment. She even felt uncomfortable at home in her own slip.

Phil had become obsessed with solving the problem of curing a flaw of Mother Nature. He worked closely with his fellow chemists and decided that her problems would go away with Dow's new breast implants. One could create the size and shape that one wanted, and then a simple operation would change a woman's shape totally. Why not his wife, beautiful in every other way? She would become a true supermodel of a wife and reflect well on him. What man would not want a woman with a perfect shape?

He raised the issue with her again, and she was negative. And he pressed the matter, but she continued to refuse. Then one day she went into his home lab, and leafed through his records of experiments that he had undertaken. She was impressed by the range and depth of his interests, for it showed a real desire to master nature. But she could not help but notice that his results were often incomplete or contradictory.

The next time he raised the question of implants, she was bold enough to talk about the success rates of his experiments. He became inflamed that she would not love him enough to trust him. She immediately apologized, but she heard again his views about himself and his mastery over nature.

Finally, for peace in the family she gave in and had the implants put in. When she left the hospital, he thought she was truly statuesque, and took her from one event to another. Her breasts looked round and ripe, and tilted upwards. At first he was afraid to even touch her for she seemed to him so beautiful.

But after a month she became suddenly sick, and the hospital doctors observed immediately an example of implants leaking. By the time they dealt with her, the saline solution had gotten into her blood stream. Phil stayed by her bedside knowing that the *right* doctors could overcome her physical ailments.

But they didn't and she kissed him gently, and then she died of septicemia.

A story adapted from Nathaniel Hawthorne's "The Birthmark."

5. A CEMETERY PLOT

On the beautiful campus of Georgetown University was the Driscoll School of Biological Sciences building, financed by the huge largesse of an alumni, class of '32. In gratitude, the great university looked the other way at its rigorous standards and let his son Devan enter its exclusive class. He was too canny to enter biomedicine, but chose instead English Literature, specializing in the works of Anthony Trollope, a prolific novelist whose work went out of style when Queen Victoria died.

Devan's main area of interest though was women, girls, widows, prepubescent teenagers—any type brought out the hunter in him. As he once said at a Georgetown mixer, "It is the chase that is the most enjoyable part of dating." He once announced that his goal in life was to bed 10,000 women before he died.

One night he and his current beloved cut through an old colonial cemetery. There were beautiful marble crypts coming out of the ground, carved with angels and little cherubs on the sides. He impulsively sat on top of one and, after very little coaxing, his paramour unzipped his pants and happily serviced him. And then they pranced away with a sense of secret achievement. A week later, they broke up—she found a boy who was even richer and he found a girl who was into bondage and sadism.

But in a few weeks he began to be plagued by terrible, violent and vivid nightmares, waking up sweating profusely and then freezing from the sweat. One night he was attacked by a red-horned devil carrying a knife, attempting to cut off his genitals.

Then a second night he was wrestling all through the darkness with a vague figure, a sort of angry angel, and the battle only ended when he awoke from the pronounced poundings of his frightened heart. One evening after a rather successful date, he walked to his dormitory in the early morning, and he was attacked near the College of Theology by a pack of grotesque dogs, demanding that he give up his soul or they would rip him apart. He was an athlete by training and overcame them by darting into the college chapel which for some reason was open that early morning.

Soon he realized that something was very wrong with his mind. At the same time as Devan was feeling these strange happenings, the university was receiving considerable publicity from a best-selling novel by William Blatty called *The Exorcist*. The book was the story of a twelve-year-old girl possessed by the devil who in the end was saved by the intervention of a Catholic priest—an exorcist—who was supposedly attending Georgetown.

Devan was close to several of the young Jesuit seminarians, and he slyly questioned them about who was the celebrity priest in the order. Finally, one told him frankly that he was off base. The priest was not a Jesuit, for they were too proud, too arrogant, too learned to engage in the "black arts" as he put it. In every Catholic diocese, the bishop apparently appoints one man to assume the role of exorcist, and his identity is kept hidden until his services are required. The modern church believed that it was best to downplay the exorcist's existence for it reminded too many skeptics about its medieval past. Yet the churchmen knew the devil and his allies truly existed. As one bishop remarked, "You students believe Nietzsche who said God is dead, but here you live in the twentieth century, and how can you not believe the devil lives? Look at his works; they have made the fabric of your world."

So the Jesuit seminarian gave him his best guess—the exorcist was not a flashy Jesuit, but a quiet, simple parish priest just studying at Georgetown but without any recognition, except from the archbishop cardinal of Washington.

Devan couldn't figure out how to even reach out to him, and then he decided to attend the 6 a.m. Mass every morning hoping to see perchance by repetition a humble priest in a pew. So for over a week he noticed one quiet, simple priest who kept coming, and finally after Mass on the seventh day Devan went up to him. "Father, will you hear my confession?"

"My son, I am only a student here, you should go to the campus ministry. They will set you up with a fine learned confessor."

"No, I want you. You can't deny my confession, can you? Let's go over there to the empty confessional."

The priest, of course, could not under canon law deny him penance, and he went with Devan into the dark confessional, flipping on the reading lamp.

Devan began, "Bless me father for I have sinned." He then began a chronicle of only a few of his sins and stopped. "Father, I am possessed by the devil, and I believe that you are the exorcist that we have all heard of. Is that not so?"

The priest stopped, and then simply said, "Yes."

Devan went on, "Please help me."

The priest replied, "It is necessary for me to get the cardinal's permission, and I think he would prefer that you try first psychoanalysis and therapy. Exorcism is so rare despite the novel."

"But that was you, wasn't it?"

"Yes, but this is bound by the secrecy of the confessional."

Devan persisted, "I ask you in the name of the spirit of the confessional to cast out the devil. Christ was asked to do that, and He did it."

"I am not Christ."

"But you represent Him in the confessional."

The priest turned off the light and obviously was troubled. Leaving the confessional, Devan promptly followed. The priest then responded, "Where do you live? On campus?"

"Yes, in New South, room 104."

"The most unruly dorm they have here. When does the devil visit you?"

"At 3 a.m. or so."

"Of course, the bewitching hour."

Devan nodded and pointed over to the College of Theology. "They came out of there one night."

The priest laughed and said, "I am happy that I am studying history instead of theology. I will meet you at your room at 2:45 a.m. I will come, rest assured. He knows me from before."

And so at 2:45 a.m. the priest appeared in his simple cassock and a Roman collar, carrying a copy of *The Latin Rite of Exorcism*. He sat down on the desk chair and said nothing to Devan, and then at 3 a.m. on the dot, the digital clock clicked and at the door appeared a devil come to do battle. He walked toward Devan and challenged him, almost angrily, at his presumption in bringing the exorcist to his room. "Tell him Devan how over the years you have compiled all these sins." And then on the wall there was a series of flashes, pictures of girls whom he had used, the two abortions, the young prepubescent girls he had foully dreamt of, the cemetery episode. Then the evil one turned to the sitting priest, "See what you are defending. Even you must have your limits. Go back, he is my disciple."

But the priest simply rose and started reading from the book. The evil one writhed and twisted in pain, but he stood his ground. The priest turned to Devan, "In the name of Christ, I absolve you of all your sins."

"You damn fool, I will see this man in hell, and you will be disgraced in front of your own cardinal. You shall not win this one. It is too obvious. He will be a patron in hell."

The priest held up his crucifix, but the devil smacked it across the room and the plastic body of Christ fell off the wooden cross. The exorcist was startled; never had that happened. But he refused to give the evil one another soul. Enough went on in the world for that. Devan was in the corner, away from the door, shaking at the episode. Then suddenly the evil one looked uneasily at the fractured crucifix and pronounced, "I will be back tomorrow night. Be ready." And he vanished.

The exorcist said nothing at all. As he left he looked at where the evil spirit had stood and noticed only some ashes on the floor. He then turned to a shaken Devan, "Tomorrow at 2:45 a.m. Okay?"

The next night the exorcist arrived, but this time in full liturgical vestments with an embroidered portrait of St. Michael on his chasuble. According to ancient Catholic tradition based on the Hebrew, it was St. Michael who defeated Lucifer and cast him forever into hell. At 3 a.m. the evil one reappeared, but this time with a powerful looking Lucifer standing by his side. He looked at the exorcist's vestments and backed off a little. The evil one called on the princes of the deep to help him, and the room was filled with ashes and feces and vomit and the body parts of other victims.

"Here exorcist, this is your humanity. Devan is just an apprentice in evil."

The exorcist stood full stature and read from his book again, but the devil stayed strong, and the smell of the filth nearly overwhelmed the gentle priest. Devan was frightened and hovered behind him for protection.

Lucifer came forward and challenged the priest to end his fragile attempts to overwhelm the natural destiny of man. "This is our time, padre. This is our century."

But the exorcist raised up a golden pix and opened it to show a consecrated host from the morning Mass, screaming, "Be gone Satan, be gone forever." And as the evil ones vanished, the exorcist took the host and placed it back in the golden pix.

Devan looked as if he had seen the worst nightmare he had ever endured, and then he thought, *this is all nonsense*. But still frozen in fear, he asked the exorcist, "Is that it? Is that the end?"

"Yes, they will never bother you again, but this experience will mark your character forever, my boy."

"But you have forgiven me, forgiven my sins. I heard you, and now they are all gone."

"Yes, I have, and they will be a bitter memory to you. But you must now pay a penance, for evil is not just an adventure."

"What can I do?"

"You can do nothing I am afraid, for you have so let evil into your life it has left a stain on your character."

"But I am forgiven. I acknowledge my thoughts and actions."

"Yes, you do, but for the rest of your life you will never know love of any type."

"But I am just a young man in search of love."

"No, you are not, you are a predator. I must leave. I am to say the 6 a.m. Mass. The Jesuits are all on an Ignaitian retreat. That's all they have, retreats, retreats. Why they just don't say the rosary every day, I don't know."

6. OUT, OUT DAMNED SPOT

To further the ideal of a well-rounded college freshman, Fairleigh Dickinson University in Madison enacted a broad curriculum with varied courses to expose students to great minds and great ideas as early as possible. In English the university required all freshmen to read Shakespeare's *Macbeth*, an interesting but superstitiously haunting play. It seemed to bring very bad luck to the major actors who performed it, which is why actors never refer to it by name, but rather as "The Scottish Play."

It was that course which most appealed and almost preoccupied Delores Fusco. She was the oldest girl in a family of five; her parents sent her to college even though she had no aptitude for academics. College was for them part of the American dream, and they scrimped and saved to afford the tuition to that over-priced institution.

Then the Fusco kids came in rapid succession, and Delores had little time to be the treasured oldest child. She received little attention, and soon ended up helping her mother on baby care and housework. She felt immediately neglected, and that sentiment etched its way into her personality. The only way she acquired attention was through tantrums, and that seemed to continued long after its due.

In school she had few friends and she was angry and depressed all the time, and her seeming possessiveness made it difficult for her to get a decent date, even among the boys of Madison who had low standards to begin with. Perhaps college would be different.

So as she read *Macbeth* over and over again, she developed a real affection for Lady Macbeth, the archvillain of the piece. What she took from that play was that Lady Macbeth started well because of her ability to control men throughout her life, and exhibited the importance of the will to prevail. Shakespeare had her unravel at the end though. At first the Bard was totally captive to her way of thinking. Lady Macbeth cajoled, screamed, yelled at her lord husband to obey her, but in the end she regretted her murders and sought to wash away the blood on her hands.

But Delores thought she did that because Shakespeare wanted to change as she said, "the fine revenge play he had written into a morality play for the church members in his audience." She wondered what if Lady Macbeth stayed strong against that old Christian ethos of guilt and ran her house as she wished. Lord Macbeth may have been the thane of the land, but "she would be queen of the household over him."

Thus she developed a compelling theory of female behavior. Women must show their strength, and force others in their lives to bend to her ways. In her freshman year she met a nice, quiet local boy, uninterested in college, whom she immediately possessed. She did what was necessary to seduce and to keep him. They married quickly, and they moved into an apartment across from her father-in-law. Her husband's mother had died early in his life, and he was unsure exactly how to deal with women and so he just put up with her antics.

They stayed married, and had seven children in a row, and when challenged about that excess, she exclaimed, "What you people don't realize is that I am a good Catholic." She came to resent the time her husband spent away from her and the family, earning money for them and still socializing briefly with his siblings. She claimed once that a relative living above her apartment had hung out his laundry, and the water from the old clothesline dripped deliberately on her head. She cut off ties with those people immediately. Then a major blow-up came. She went to a family shower and gave the fiancée a gift, but nobody made a big deal about it. Such offenses were major slights in the vocabulary of Italian-American women, so she stopped talking to anybody in that group and demanded that her husband do so as well.

When the eldest sister of her husband tried to reach out and at Easter sent her two daughters with a beautiful pizzagaina as a peace offering to her, Dolores opened the door, looked at them, and threw it in their faces. "Out, out you hypocrites. Get out." And she started banging her head against the wall near the door. Was she insane, they asked? In fear, they never talked to her again.

She also alienated her own immediate family, and demanded that her poor husband stand by her. When she sued her eldest daughter in open court for the return of a worn-out coffee table, she demanded that in the ignominious dispute her husband appear in court against his own daughter. The judge was flabbergasted for he knew the husband and admired him, and in Italian-American families, fathers do not sue their children. But she won, she got the table back and experienced the triumph of justice against her own child.

As her seven kids grew up, she filled them with a steady diet of malice, especially against their father's family. She sat in the back of the church on Sundays at the 9 a.m. Mass, and her eyes bored into the back of the heads of her husband's siblings. Her husband's family thus received the cold treatment which they called the *malocchio* or the evil eye, stronger than even that of the most powerful witch in town.

As she got older, she got more haggard and gray, developed diabetes and lost 40 pounds. People rarely recognized her.

As her own children grew up, she became stranger and harsher, and her husband had to work two jobs to support her ambitions and the needs of his children. He also began to feel the pains of old age, and it was unclear if he were suffering more from his aches and pains or from the huge amount of powerful medications that the doctors put him on. One day while she was shopping, he lay sick in bed and took the phone into his room, and began to call his siblings with whom he had been forbidden to communicate.

They talked of old times, of gentle grandma and of crusty grandpa, and of each other's follies, and he for the first time in so long seemed to have a good time. To one brother, he finally lamented that he had spent his whole adult life with her, and then clinically observed, "This is the problem when you marry the first girl you sleep with." When he died, half of his children did not come to the funeral. It was not out of disrespect, but because they had become so alienated from Delores over the years of arguments. At the wake four sons looked out sourly at the crowd. The husband's oldest living sister, Margaret, shuffled slowly up the aisle with her cane, said her prayers for her long-lost brother whom she loved dearly, and then heroically went over to the children. She quietly looked at each of them and said, "I am your aunt. I'm sorry." Not a single one acknowledged her, for Delores had done her training in hatred and spite very well. No one knew what Lady Macbeth had promised the older children, but it was a heritage of spite, of hatred, and of possessiveness, and that training changed not only the play, but also her life.

7. RESURRECTION

Josh O'Connell still lived with his family in a three-decker home in Dorchester and worked in the rare books section of the Boston Public Library on Copley Square. He was a quiet, unassuming fellow and able to enjoy solitude for long stretches of time. His mother was a housekeeper in the city, and his father worked as a watchman of the so-called Sister Corita gas towers covered with paint streaks designed by the nun.

Josh's major source of enjoyment was to continue on the Red Line and transfer to the Green Line in order to watch the Boston Red Sox play at Fenway Park. Usually he bought the cheapest seats he could, directly behind the huge green wall. When he got off the subway stop, he would amble up the side street, over the bridge, and onto Yawkey Way. The way was named after the legendary racist owner of the Red Sox who opposed integration to the extent that he even refused to acquire the legendary Willie Mays.

On the way to the park Josh passed endless seedy bars, guys selling non-copyrighted hats and shirts at half the price that the league wanted, and a huge black lady selling peanuts at a dollar a bag. They had somehow been roasted that very day and were truly delicious, Further up the street Josh always gave money to an old nun dressed in a gray habit with her eyes closed and a bowl with some change and dollars in it. She never acknowledged anyone's gift, never even opened her heavy eyelids. Josh would give her a dollar before every game and by the fifth inning she was gone.

Then in an impulsive way one afternoon, he came down the road and dropped his dollar in her bowl, and said quietly to the nun, "Do not fear, the judgment is at hand." She opened her eyes, rose, and gave him her bowl and her seat. He was now in charge, he guessed! After the game, he dropped the money off in the poor box at St. Mary's Church in Dorchester. Every time he walked by her on the way to the park he thought of her dedication and became more and more intent on learning the stories of Jesus Christ in the New Testament. He was not so involved in the teachings as much as the miracle stories of which there are about thirty or so, including the famous resurrection of Lazarus, the healing of the blind and deaf, and the multiplication of the fishes and loves. He was fascinated by Christ's prediction that he would return soon, and that his disciples in the meantime should go out and teach all peoples.

He began to wonder if he too had been given the prophet's gifts, and commenced praying extensively for such powers. One day he was back at the ballpark entrance, and he saw a wheelchair bound little girl who was just sitting there waiting for her parents to park their car.

Josh went up to her and smiled, and then abruptly commanded her, "Rise up girl. The Kingdom's at hand." The begging nun looked on in disbelief as the little girl did as she was told. She rose up, holding on to the chair's railing and sharply looked at him. How much she could walk already, he did not know, but he regarded her standing as a healing episode. She smiled so brightly that even the old nun was overwhelmed by her sentiment.

Then a week later, he left the rare books section of the library, went across the street to the magnificent Trinity Episcopal church designed by H. H. Richardson, and joined the long soup line feeding the many hungry. As he watched for hours, the kitchen began to run out of soup, but not out of the poor. He ventured over to the elegant Copley Plaza Hotel kitchen and went through the back doors. Josh spotted a huge pot of New England clam chowder, and he signaled authoritatively to a Hispanic worker to grab the other end and walk with him to the church. Suddenly the line had gone from donating mere drippings to feed the poor and hungry to a full pot of soup—New England style clam chowder it turned out. Soon the Copley Plaza chefs were desperately looking for their daily soup, but somehow it vanished! Joshua had begun to multiply the loaves and the fishes.

He began standing in the small park in front of the church and the hotel, preaching, for he had come to realize that Jesus was not just a miracle man, but a teacher and his disciples were prophets of the coming future. People began to gather, bringing sick children and aching old people near the end of their time. He told them all, "The Kingdom is at hand. Don't look up or down. Do not look at churches or shrines; the Kingdom is inside of you. You possess the Lord, and where three of you gather together to pray, even if you are strangers, He is among you."

Then one smart-ass college kid cried out, "Tell us, what is the essence of your gospel, prophet?"

"It is simple and short. Love God and love your neighbor, even if you hate him, for love and mercy are the center of the Good News."

"Why is there so much evil in our times, prophet?"

"We cannot by ourselves defeat evil. Pray to Jesus and remember your task is to worry about your own soul."

And he stopped and paraphrased the beatitudes of old, "Blessed are the poor, blessed are the weak, blessed are the peacemakers. Remember well, we do not ask for an eye for an eye, but for mercy. And if you have two coats in this Boston winter, stand here with me and give one away. For look at the lilies of the field; they neither sow nor reap, but they are more elegant than the Kingdom of Solomon in all its glory. They call me the prophet, but it is you who are prophets of God. Stand close, stand alone, and at home and at work, preaching the Good News. Yes, you will be taken advantage of, and called naïve and foolish, but speak Jesus' words even to the jaded, even to the hypocrites. Be as pleasant as a dove, but as a wily as a serpent. Share your goods with each other, and remember you cannot inherit the new Kingdom. You will leave as you came

in, naked and afraid. The Kingdom is around you and you have it inside of you."
One cold night, he attracted a large crowd and proclaimed to them strange words.

I asked God to take away my pride, and God said, "NO".
He said it was not for Him to take it away, but for me to give it up.

I asked God to make my handicapped child whole, and God said, "NO".
He said her spirit is whole, her body is only temporary.

I asked God to grant me patience, and God said, "NO."
He said that patience is a by-product of tribulation, it isn't granted, it's earned.

I asked God to give me happiness, and God said, "NO."
He said He gives blessings, happiness is up to me.

I asked God to spare me pain, and God said, "NO".
He said suffering draws you apart from worldly cares, and brings you closer to me.

I asked God to make my spirit grow, and He said, "NO".
He said I must grow on my own, but He will prune me to make me fruitful.

I asked God to help me love others as much as He loves me,
And God said, "Ah, finally you have the idea!"

And the crowd listened, but some walked away for it was too strange a message to live by in this world. The archdiocese sent an observer to quietly hear the prophet, and he reported back that the prophet preached the familiar words of the gospel, but he taught that God was in one's heart and not in the churches. He could easily put them out of business, and they asked the Irish cops to push him along and harass his gatherings.

One night back at home in Dorchester, he heard the commotion of large, angry gangs of Patriots and Champions, fully armed with guns and knives and billy clubs, fighting over territory for their drug trafficking. Josh ran down from the triple-decker where he lived and headed straight to the center of the two groups, dressed only in his old bathrobe and carrying a copy of the Bible. He demanded that they halt and lay down their weapons. The hardened warriors stared at him. He was crazy. This was their territory, their livelihoods.

He began, "I implore you in the name of Christ Jesus to lay down your weapons and end all the battles. Go home and live in peace. Nothing is to be gained by this violence. Tomorrow you will begin again, and the next day even more, and the next week after. Go back to your families. Go back to your mothers. You have nothing to prove. This territory belongs to all of us. This is the neighborhood created by God." And when he finished they moved around him, and together started beating him with their butt handles, and one thug stepped on his copy of the Bible as if it were street trash. When he came to, Joshua was in an ambulance headed to Mass General Hospital with a severe concussion and several broken ribs. He was released in a week and went back to the rare book section. There by coincidence he found a photocopy of the Dead Sea scrolls, and rediscovered the wisdom of the teacher of righteousness. He was like Jesus, but he was more gentle, more open to female leadership, more dedicated to the secret wisdom of the Gnosis.

Perhaps this was Josh's mistake, that he had short-changed the teachings of Christ. He did not preach so much of the Kingdom and the hearts of men and women. And he began to think more of how to explain the greatest aspects of God to all. He went back to the small park and began anew, "And so I say to you, love your enemies, embrace all differences as one, for there is no male or female, no Jew or Gentile, no citizen or stranger. All are one in our Kingdom. To those who are violent, chastise them not. But know they crucified the Lord. Oh, forgive them for they know not what they do."

And as he spoke night after night, the crowds grew again and ended their meetings with the prayer that the Lord had taught His own disciples.

Then one night the Boston cops got tired of the crowds and listening to the message of the prophet. They arrested him for disturbing the peace, and pulled him into the district precinct house. And as in the good old days, they tied him in a chair and put electrodes on his body. They began shock treatments, but did not stop when they should have. They seemed to enjoy the pleasure of pain or watching him writhe, but he said little. Then he gave up his spirit. He had a massive heart attack and died. The police chief was afraid of the consequences for this was not the good old days anymore. The rank and file police quietly took his body to a faraway cemetery in a remote area of Chelsea and quickly buried him there. And then they threw fast-growing grass seed on the spot, and for several days stood guard so that nobody would disturb the grass. There was no headstone or gravesite, so no one would know where the prophet was buried, even for all eternity.

8. CONFESSION

"Blessed me, father, for I have sinned—it has been 10 years since my last confession."

The priest looked through the grill and could barely make out a fairly young man. Usually on Saturday afternoons he only heard in confession old Italian ladies who had sworn at their neighbors. He responded, "Glad to have you home again, son. What do you wish to confess?"

"I have not been to confession since my parents took me in Sicily. Now I come to ask a peculiar request, I wish to be forgiven for murdering my wife."

"You murdered your wife!"

"No, I am planning to and I want to make sure that God in His mercy will forgive me when it is done."

"Confession doesn't work like that. And why would you want to commit such a terrible crime?"

"I have found out that the putana is sleeping with my best friend. They meet every Wednesday at noon at the Peter Pan hotel down the road. She's playing me for a stooge, a cuckold. My honor requires that I end this infamy."

"Have you talked to her, maybe there is misunderstanding. "

"She supposedly is going shopping, but after an hour, she returns with a gallon of milk."

"You can't kill your wife, you must talk to her."

"I want to know, will I be forgiven? Why should I go to hell for her sins?"

"No, no this is confusing. You should go home and talk to her after this visit. And then come to me before you do anything."

"Are you going to give me forgiveness now?"

"You have committed no sin except the worst evil thoughts. Push aside those thoughts and then come back to me." And so the young man left the confessional, and the priest just sat there in total surprise.

Two weeks later, the priest was still thinking about the weird encounter, so he decided to go on Wednesday at noon to the parking lot of the hotel that rented rooms by the month, the week, the day or the hour. And sure enough at noon, he saw a pickup truck from Massie's construction there, and next to it slid a Toyota with an attractive girl coming out. The priest waited there, and for an hour there was no one departing, and then they left hand-in-hand quickly.

About ten days later, he was reading the *Buffalo Evening News*, and there the lead story was that a husband had killed his wife, claiming she was committing adultery in his very bed. The prosecutor immediately brought the case to the jury, but the panel of seven men and two women found that he was innocent by virtue of temporary insanity. As the foreman said to the reporters, "What man would not do the same?" So the murderer went free, and went back to work at the construction site.

Two months later, the priest was in the confessional, quietly reading his breviary, a daily prayer book for the religious, and he heard some rattling in the confessional. He opened the sliding window, and saw a familiar face.

"Blessed me, father, It is has been a few months since my last confession. I have only one sin, I killed my adulterous wife. "

The priest responded, "I thought the jury found you not guilty by virtue of insanity."

"No, I was guilty; I killed her and her lover with knowledge of what I was doing. I just didn't think it would be in my bed. I had to buy a new mattress."

"But the jury…"

"It doesn't matter now, for in the eyes of the law I have been found not guilty and cannot be tried again under the Constitution. They call it double jeopardy."

"And you are here, why?"

"Because I wish to be absolved of the murder. You constantly talk about God as a Being of mercy, one whose forgiveness knows no bounds. I wish for mercy for my sins."

The priest was a bit taken back by this man's calculation. "I cannot see how you can expect me to absolve you since I knew what you were going to do before you did it. "

"It doesn't matter, I demand mercy and you cannot as a priest not forgive my sins."

"And what am I supposed to tell you?"

"Also, I should mention that I am engaged to a girl who knows the whole story, well most of it. And we want you to officiate at the wedding. You have meant so much to my life, father."

The priest was horrified, "I think that you might want to use her parish priest, that is the normal way."

"No, she has no parish; she is Catholic but in name only. Not like me. Besides we feel that we want to name the first baby boy after you. Also since this is my second marriage, can we skip the Cana conference stuff?"

9. HITTING THE HIGH "C"

When grandma died, the weekly Sunday dinners rotated to her eldest daughter, Mary, who was a determined organized woman, and who at sixteen insisted on marrying her first cousin. The family opposed the union vigorously, and the Catholic Church had a rule against such marriages. But she insisted, and the local church applied for a dispensation from the Vatican, and it was granted. They stayed married for fifty years, had four children, and moved from one interesting house in Madison to another.

One day looking out the large kitchen window, Mary claimed she saw the Virgin Mary appearing near the garden and moving slowly through the grasses. She told no one except her husband. In honor of both of them, he built an ingenious shrine to the Blessed Mother. He took a white porcelain tub, propped it up, surrounded it with stones and rocks, and lovingly placed in the grotto a statue of the Immaculate Conception. Some of the family members made fun of it, but it was his way of bringing Italian piety to his new multi-gabled Victorian house.

One Sunday Mary decided to invite not just the regular members of the immediate family, but also some distant relatives from North Street, the earlier Italian neighborhood in Madison. One of the guests was a charming twenty-five-year-old singer, George Esposito, who was just beginning his career as a fine tenor. After the six course Italian dinner, she gathered her guests in her large living room, introduced Esposito, and asked him to sing for the family. Nobody was much interested in being a captive audience, but when he began the old ladies compared him to the great tenor Mario Lanza.

He began with an aria from *Tosca*, then went into *O Sole Mio*, and asked the guests to sing with him the song, *Funiculì, Funiculà*. Esposito quickly went through some Dean Martin songs, the most popular being of course the silly *Hey Marie*, "you gotta get up, we need the sheets for the table."

Then Mary reminded everyone that George was going to appear on the Ted Mack Amateur Hour in a month, and people from all over the nation were to send in penny postcards judging which of the acts was the very best. We were to get together and sign as many cards as we could, and she rushed over and handed out the cards to us. We were to vote before we saw the show, but she would not mail them herself to the CBS studios until the day after he appeared. There was probably something wrong with her prescription, but after all, he was family. La famiglia was all that counted.

27

Well, George won, and his prize was a spot on the Ed Sullivan television show. Sullivan was a Broadway columnist for the *New York Daily News*, had a rigid personality, but had a marvelous ability to garner talent. His show later made Elvis Presley and the Beatles famous to all America.

George went on to sing a Lanza favorite, *Be My Love*, which had sold over a million records for the venerated tenor from Philadelphia. The reaction was enormous and respectful, and George captured the audience which allowed him to be in many cases the introductory act before the great talents appearing in different shows, like Martin and Lewis, George Burns and Gracie Allen, Bob Hope, and even the magnificent Sinatra who once graciously called the young singer "his protégé."

For years George traveled the roads across the country, earning a good salary, meeting important people in Las Vegas and in Hollywood, enjoying the hospitality of the mob bosses and hot show girls. It went on for years and his voice held out, and he especially enjoyed hitting the high C, the gold standard for great tenors.

One night he was booked for the early show at the Trenton War Memorial Auditorium in New Jersey, and after the performance the hosts insisted on taking him to Princeton for dinner. Trenton did not have a single good restaurant, so they ended up at the Yankee Doodle Taproom in the Nassau Inn across from the great university.

George had quit school at tenth grade and had worked as a gardener before he hit the road. He was overwhelmed by the gothic beauty of the campus. After dinner he walked the side streets, and Esposito saw a vacant store that used to be a French restaurant when Princeton had more pretensions than even now. He immediately saw its potentialities as a Italian dining place with music. He could finally settle down, raise a family, and become even better known in a smaller world.

George created a club called "Spaghetti and the Opera House" which soon became a trendy in-spot off the Route 1 corridor. The restaurant was packed, especially on weekends, and one evening Aunt Mary convinced one of her reluctant children to drive her to Princeton, all the way down from Madison, the center of her universe. At the club, George pulled her away as she came in and kissed her, saying she made all this possible. She responded that all she wanted was for him to sing for her that night *Ave Maria*, the great song in praise of the Virgin. He dismissed it, saying it was not appropriate for a dining club, but in typical fashion she persisted and he gave in, saying, "Ladies and gentlemen, tonight a special request from a special lady, *Ave Maria*." And he sang the hymn and the crowd was simply overwhelmed. Somehow they remembered it from their childhood and enjoyed it once again. Mary was delighted and that night on the way home, she said a rosary for George.

He went back to his apartment on Nassau Street, sat down, and quietly suffered a heart attack and died. He was only fifty-four. Aunt Mary lived to nearly her one-hundredth birthday, quietly saying her rosary.

10. PETER PAN MOTEL

Somewhere near Tonawanda, New York, there used to be the stark Peter Pan Motel which had signs that told it all. You could rent a room by the week, the day, or the hour. It had cable, HBO, and a large number of vacancies. The one hour special for quick liaisons was $69 an hour. One of the frequent patrons was Alexander Girrard III, the grandson of the famous illustrator; he was the current police chief of the town. He was married to an events coordinator, June Girrard, who he said was as cold as the Buffalo spring. They had been married for fifteen years, had two children, and after a few years drifted apart, each into their own sphere of life.

Alex had fallen under the charms of a younger, red-headed dietitian and saved Wednesdays afternoon mostly for her. Once in the hotel room, which he paid cash for, they literally ripped their clothes off each other, groped on a made bed, and looked like rabbits rather than sleeping owls. The woman had originally come from Argentina, and she knew techniques and practices that enthralled Alex. After the sixth time, they lay carefully together in each other's sweat, and then she left the room first, and he followed five minutes later. He usually parked his blue Volkswagen in the back of the motel. Of all the times they were together he told her, "This was the very best." What she thought was a mystery.

Alex's wife June was not usually concerned about his times away from home. In her job, she had attracted, at the country club, the interest of the golf pro who was teaching Alex to hit long drives and to putt. Alex was a lousy golfer, and the pro wondered if he were as lousy in bed. The pro was attracted to June, who was frankly striking in some ways in her carriage. He would ask her to lunch at the club, just two employees discussing club matters together. Gradually he became bolder, and she became receptive. Like all women, she shared her thoughts with her "special friend." Mostly she was afraid she was unacceptable in bed, no matter with whom. Her friend told her quietly what men especially liked, and then handed her a dog-eared copy of Alex Comfort's *The Joy of Sex*, a virtual encyclopedia of everything that one should know about that harsh subject.

So it was that the golf pro and June decided to meet frequently in the pro's locked office, and then one day he ushered her into his red Corvette and drove to the Peter Pan Motel. They spent two hours of horseplay together. At the unceremonious end, he simply closed the door to room 108, and they left together. At the same time, Alex was getting in his car and saw them holding hands.

What was this, that cheap whore was cheating on him with his golf instructor? What a double betrayal! That night Alex had his way with her, and continued all through the darkness. Boy, he thought, she learned more from that golf pro than he ever did about putting.

Alex thought that he had been superb, what June thought was not recorded. But a month later, Alex's grandfather died, and he left his only relative a respectable fortune. Now Alex disliked his grandfather, regarding him as an interior decorator for the idle rich, and his grandfather considered Alex a disappointment, characterizing him as "a non-ambitious lunch pail." But in the end he was the sole and lucky heir.

Alex quickly put the fortune into a holding company run by Blackstone. In some ways, money changed his life in unexpected directions, that he did not at first fully recognize. Initially, he continued his life under a different corporate name, and he surreptitiously bought the Peter Pan Motel, and poured into Room 104 bedbugs and roaches when his wife and her golf pro came back for another afternoon delight; they were disgusted at the bug infestation that climbed all over them, into their clothes laying casually on the floor, and into their very shoes. June screamed loudly, grabbed her clothes and ran nearly naked out of the room, and the golf pro followed her into his Corvette. All the way home they could still feel the bugs on them, and she ran back into her house, partially undressed, straight toward the shower. Her husband watched the whole episode with delight, and he came home nonchalantly later, asking her where she was all day. She simply stood in her bathrobe, saying she was getting a cold and took a hot shower.

Two months later the Peter Pan Motel was fumigated and then leveled. Soon the land was sold for $1.00 to the Faith Christian Baptist Church which assumed it was a meaningful gift from God to further their fundamentalist ministry. As for himself, Alex helped raise the $2 million necessary for a chapel, a school, and a community house. The mostly black community thought he was a genuine white hero.

Meanwhile his wife became increasingly annoyed at his social work, and began divorce procedures to happily marry the golf pro. She never did an audit though of Alex's true wealth, and only asked for the home which he completely settled on.

The country club board began to see Alex as a true Erie County leader, and put him on the board. His first objective though was to fire the golf pro, saying that he was a poor instructor. The pro left for a post in Syracuse, and June expected to follow him, but he went solo.

Alex's work became more philanthropic and less civic, and he was the featured marshal at the town's Fourth of July parade, wearing a red, white and blue vest and a straw hat. He saluted the people from a fire truck. Children from the Faith Christian School began to file along the sidewalk and they waved their little flags proudly at him.

The town began to realize that these random acts of kindness came from an unknown foundation which was somehow controlled by Alex. Most importantly he became a bastion of decency and a noble local statesman.

Most impressive was his response when a group of town thugs desecrated the oldest Jewish cemetery in the region. He sat at a testimonial dinner one night and listened quietly as Rabbi Joel Epstein soulfully related the destruction of his people's memories. Some of those descendants had relations who had died in the Holocaust and were remembered only respectfully in prayer.

Alex was genuinely moved, and two weeks later he and a group of volunteer policemen showed up with the rabbi to set the cemetery aright. They did an adequate job, but Alex asked permission to surround the cemetery with an elegant bronze fence to protect it forever. The rabbi concurred, but then Alex put in an expensive first-rate security system directly connected to the local police department. Alex had noticed that in his grandfather's papers was a draft of a sculpture of King Solomon, the builder of the last temple in Jerusalem. Alex hired an old Italian sculptor from Buffalo who crafted the statue and placed it in the center of the cemetery, overlooking his people. The rabbi wept.

The rabbi insisted that the local synagogues hold a feast day of prayer for Alex, and he told the audience the story of the statue and the expensive security system, and then he pronounced, "Finally someone who cares about the Jewish people. Do you know Alexander what we call such people? We call them 'righteous gentiles', and you are one of such friends."

Alex proudly went home, and reviewed in his mind this deep honor and experienced the proud sense that his life finally had meaning.

11. A YANKEE BAPTISM

In celebration of our class of 1958, I initiated the fiftieth reunion of St. Vincent Martyr Elementary School and was startled at the high rate of attendance. Usually, reunions attract wealthy matrons who have kept in touch with each other. Almost every woman I talked to about the logistics of the reunion wanted to know, "Is Timmy coming?" I obediently told them he had sent in his response saying, "I will come happily." Timmy Martin was a tall, handsome, almost charismatic figure, even at the age of fourteen, and he attracted women like filaments to a magnet. I liked him as did others. He came from a fairly traditional Catholic family, and his bespectacled mother taught us in fourth grade.

But he went to the local parochial high school where he was surrounded by many temptations, the most powerful being Johnny Walker. He spent the summer as a bartender to make spending money for Bailey-Ellard Catholic High School. But one day the owner bluntly remarked that he was drinking more of the stuff than the customers. He not only fired him, but he also generously enrolled him in Alcoholics Anonymous where the regimen worked. Tim then went to a Jesuit retreat and became fascinated with St. Ignatius' prayers designed to let him feel, see, hear, and smell the crucifixion of Jesus Christ.

We heard that Timmy joined the Jesuit order in New York City after going to Fordham University and was sent for further study to the prestigious Angelicum in Rome. There he majored in canon law and was drenched in the teachings of the great theologian St. Thomas Aquinas.

Somehow Timmy vanished off the radar screen, and I was startled to get a message before the reunion that he wished to meet with me. He suggested the Yankee Doodle Taproom in the Nassau Inn across from Princeton University. When I arrived he was there already, still tall and handsome with graying hair and a Roman collar and the same eager smile I remembered. We shook hands and then sat down. At first I was a bit uncomfortable, but he began almost immediately saying, "I have tried for years to find you, but you have moved around so much." He told me the stories of wearisome girlfriends, alcohol, the AA, his scholarly interests and priestly commitment, and his career in the demanding religious order.

It was a fascinating journey, and I listened closely to it, but then sharply I asked him, "What is your plan for the year?" One of the vows of the AA is to apologize to people you have hurt in the past, and he felt that I was one of them. I realized suddenly that he was apologizing about being a bit aloof to me even in the eighth grade. "There is really no need for an apology," I said uncomfortably.

"Yes, I want to finally apologize to you. You are the last person on my list."

I just nodded and ironically tried to conclude on an up note, "You are forgiven Father!" He laughed and for two hours we talked about the past, the state of the Church, and what he studied at the college he attended in Rome. It was a different world. He said he had read my two-volume history of the presidency and enjoyed it, but thought that I had overrated Franklin Delano Roosevelt. Timmy's family was good Madison GOP stock.

Then out of the clear blue, I asked him a question that I had thought about often. "Isn't it true that the lay people like me can perform baptism without a priest being present?"

"Well, if it is an emergency and not just a curiosity, you can. But just to do it is 'illicit'."

"What is illicit? Jesus said one must be born of water and the Holy Spirit, and He Himself was baptized by John when he was thirty. When the bishops of Poland and the communist satellite in Czechoslovakia ran out of priests, they consecrated holy women to be priests. The Vatican called that *illicit* too!"

"Yeah, exactly, it was a violation of Church law."

"But they performed Mass, baptized kids, married couples, there were women priests."

"Yes, their actions were illicit, but not invalid," he professorially explained.

"But how can that be?"

"The Church has its ways. Rome has spoken." We continued on and left with a hug. There in the Taproom in a Roman collar and a black suit, he blessed me. I watched him as he walked away with the usual spring in his step. We met each other then briefly at the reunion, but I had to fight off the wealthy matrons from Madison, New Jersey. Many never knew that Timmy had married...the Church.

That same year I went to Yankee Stadium, an environment that I had loved since I was twelve-years-old. In the very first game my father took me to, I watched the rookie slugger Al Kaline of Detroit, and I was amazed at the huge space of the house that Ruth built. It had room for over 68,000 people, but the seats that were tight in the 1920s had grown even smaller as our behinds grew larger. I had come for Old-Timers' Day for years, and went on one occasion to the World Series which the Yankees had a history of winning in those days.

Some friends went with me, and one brought his grandson whom I really enjoyed. He was a little guy who loved the game. He played it, watched it on TV, and like me as a boy, memorized the statistics, for baseball is a compendium of numbers. I would try to trick him, "Who hit the second highest number of home runs after Babe Ruth in the old days?"

He knew the answer—Jimmy Foxx. "Ruth has 714 and Fox had 534." Most people named "Hank Greenberg."

He was a fine boy, except his parents were atheists, and he was never baptized. Even if he died with no major sin, he would go to a place called Limbo and never see the Divine Presence. Limbo was until recently defined as a pleasant place for the unbaptized good people but not heaven. It was none of my business, but it bothered me. I soon became more and more concerned about the fate of the boy. I turned to his grandfather who laughed at me, and said, "An educated man like you shouldn't believe in that crap." But I became increasingly fixated on the boy and questioned his innocent fate.

The next year, we again all met at Yankee Stadium for the Old-Timers' Day. It was a long day and after the Old-Timers' salute, I offered to buy the boy a hotdog and a Coke, and he gladly came with me.

The lines were long, and finally I ordered for him and asked the attendant to just give me a courtesy cup with some water so that I could take a prescription pill. He nonchalantly gave me one and we moved on to the condiments section which was packed. And then in a quick move, I poured a tiny stream of water over the boy's crown. I said to myself, "I baptize you in the name of the Father, the Son, and the Holy Ghost."

"Hey, one of those people just poured a Coke on me," he protested.

"Ah, don't worry about it. It is a real zoo here today." We went back to our seats and saw the regular game. No Limbo for him. There his grandfather answered they were leaving the regular game at the seventh inning and taking a cab together to Grand Central Station. Fine, I was taking the subway outside the stadium to Columbus Circle and then down to Penn Station. It would be a parting of the ways prematurely.

The railroad went back home to Summit which is only a short 45 minutes from Penn Station. But when I arrived, both of my parents were there to meet me. They looked ashen and disturbed. I got out of the car and asked what was wrong. Mom turned soberly and said, "Jim and his friend got in a very bad taxi accident. They are in a hospital in serious condition. The little boy had no seat belt on and went through the window. The cab driver hit an Armour meat truck on Bruckner Boulevard. They never had a chance."

I was flabbergasted, startled, and then deeply somber. That night the boy's grandmother called me. She was an Italian-born widow, and he was her only grandchild, and her only child was in the hospital. Would I help her with the arrangements? I went to Ippoliti's Funeral Home and Paul sold her, of course, the most expensive package, and she, in a daze, approved it. We went then to the rectory of St. Theresa Catholic Church in Summit and arranged a funeral. The priest was amiable enough, and then remarked, "Of course, he was baptized?"

Grandma looked what the Italians call *stunad*, but I quickly answered, "Yes, of course, in fact I was the godparent."

"Oh good, we don't have to check it out if you say so." And then the boy was laid to rest in consecrated ground. According to our theology, he was innocent and went directly to heaven. But I had committed, it seemed, a violation of canon law. And I asked a priest friend years later, what I could do, he was understandably blunt.

"You showed the sense of pride by violating the authority of the Church. That can be forgiven, but I am afraid you exhibited disrespect for the Holy

Ghost, and Jesus said that that was the only sin that could not be forgiven."

"But I in fact showed respect for the Holy Ghost, and even mentioned His name."

"But you did this illicit baptism in His name."

"That makes no sense, I permitted the kid to go to heaven just before his death. And now for doing that I myself will go to hell."

"You violated the rules of the Church. It is a tough policy, but it is that way." A year later I read the diary of a mystic Polish nun named St. Faustina about the mercy of God in which she includes her conversations with Jesus. In it He says that all sins are forgivable, and the worse sinners command His special mercy, and He was thus committed more to them. And so I counted on this admonition for a strange situation, not assured of God's justice, but of His mercy.

Yet, on Old-Timers' Day every year I would show up at the stadium, getting seats on the end of the aisle. Leaving one seat vacant, I would remember the boy and lean over to his place, talking of Mantle, Berra, the "Moose"... But he never answered me.

12. CONFUCIUS SAYS

The word travel is a derivative of travail, hard work, and most arduous for me in so many ways is air travel. I have really tried to avoid long air travel, especially to Asia, a minimum fourteen hours straight from the east coast to the Orient. My college had a long-standing agreement with a medical school in Tianjin, once a famed port city of Peking, and they wanted it renewed in person. Like most of the Communist Chinese urban areas, it looked both new and run down, with an architectural style that lacked class and elegance. Aluminum and glass, shapeless and utilitarian. The elegance in the area can be seen in the oldest part of the cities, especially Beijing with its emperors' palaces and huge ballrooms and public spaces.

I frankly avoided the trip for two years of my college presidency because of the travel ordeal, but finally I was gently informed that the Chinese educators were losing "face" with their colleagues because I never showed up. They even promised me an honorary doctorate in medicine from the university. My mother had always wanted me to be a doctor, and was disappointed when what I got at age 25 was a doctorate in political science. So I went from Logan Airport to JFK and then to Detroit to China, an even more circuitous route than usual.

The reception at the airport was extraordinary. I just wanted to accept greetings and then go right to sleep, but they planned a fourteen-course meal signifying my high status in their eyes. The Chinese are a formal, but hospitable, people with a long tradition of welcoming foreigners, usually invaders. The next morning I looked out the hotel window and saw an ocean of Chinese white collar workers on their way to work on bicycles. The street was a Garden State Parkway for two wheelers.

I met with public authorities, party members, composed an arrangement with the medical university and was surrounded by television cameras and newspaper reporters. I felt like Nixon visiting Mao. At the same time, I humbly thought that it made more sense for them to have agreements with the leaders of Johns Hopkins or Columbia Presbyterian than us.

They insisted I see the sights of the capital for the next four days. I huffed up the Great Wall, the only structure on earth that can be seen from outer space. A newly married couple came up to me and insisted that the husband take a picture of me and his wife together. As we stood there aimlessly, I felt her squeezing my behind. Was this some sort of ritual for new brides?

We made our way to endless lovely palaces and ended up one day at the

Summer Palace on a moored boat made out of cement. A group of Chinese children surrounded me as if I were a television celebrity, and one little guy said in broken English, "You look like my grandfather."

My Achilles heel in traveling is my dislike of Chinese food, even in the assimilated U.S. style. I would smile, push the food around on my plate, and after a day or so they would take me to a special place for breakfast— McDonald's. We arrived early in the morning and there was a sign saying it was closed for the week. They promised me that we would have lunch in a special food court which had some thirty booths. Unfortunately, it was from thirty different regions of China, not a burger in sight. We went to the small eating store for the province of Shantung.

They whispered and pointed at the proprietor who was humbly washing dishes and could be seen through the kitchen door. Finally I wanted to know what the commotion was. The guide of mine said he was the descendent of the great Chinese philosopher Confucius. I wanted to be introduced to the 76th direct descendent in his line, and out came a diffident smiling man who put his arm around my waist as the guides took pictures of the union.

I wondered if Confucius looked like him. Did the illustrious forebear have features like this? I graciously remarked, "You have great blood in your veins." I was told that there was no finer compliment that could be paid, especially by a Westerner. Then quietly he took me in the back storage room alone, and there was a magnificent gown in gold with Chinese characters written on it. Later a guide told me that the characters said, "A man is wise when he knows the state of his ignorance." Sounded like Socrates.

That night I stood outside my hotel and in the blazing street lights and neon signs, I saw him walking quickly up the avenue. He went into a nondescript building that had a sign in English, "Confucius Studies Center." I followed him a bit excited, and my two guides across the street, obviously party agents, followed me quietly.

Inside was a group of twenty elderly Chinese men, many looking like scholars from bygone years, and he came in and was accepted as a hero. He unrolled a small scroll that I was told later had some of the "Analects of Confucius." He started extrapolating from the text, like a Methodist minister in Kentucky reading from the epistles of St. Paul. I quickly left and turned around to see the two guides exit with the scholar, one guide on each side, each dressed in a cheap black gabardine suit. His face in the neon lights knew fear, and his gown sparkled in the fake light of the center of the city.

MICHAEL P. RICCARDS

13. CLOWN COLLEGE

High above the city of Boston, John Xavier Reilly had his offices in the Prudential Tower. Like most boys from the middle class, he had struggled to become terribly wealthy, for no particular reason than to be rich beyond his youthful dreams. And he was, and had three sons whom he wanted to go even further than he had, for wasn't that the definition of the American Dream?

The first son was a graduate of Harvard Medical and was now the youngest chief surgeon in the cardiac unit. The second was a graduate of Yale Law School and was a junior partner of Foley, Hoag, and Elliot, the premier white shoe law firm in New England. And his last son seemed to have less ambition, but he loved to put things together, and through Reilly's pull he was admitted to mechanical engineering at MIT.

In his third year, he went on midsemester break to Florida to get away from the Boston winter, and his group ended up at Sarasota. There one day they visited the Ringling Brothers, Barnum and Bailey headquarters which had attached to it a beautiful museum of impressionist art which the circus fortune had apparently bought at the height of its greatness. The third son, Philip, was fascinated by the collection, and walking down the gravel road past the beautiful tropical trees, he stopped at the circus museum. There in the structure honoring the age-old circus traditions going back to Europe, he saw pictures, customs, and memorabilia that honored the august history of the circus as a way of life.

While he was there, he stopped in a side cubicle that was the admissions office of the Clown College with a list of its training programs and elective courses in magic, children's tricks, and a variety of other interesting activities they conducted. One could not just be a clown as in the Middle Ages, but now you were trained in its subtle arts of humor, tumbling, and crowd pleasing movements. Philip was fascinated with its curriculum, and took the application materials back to Boston.

When he graduated from MIT, his father pulled all his strings to get his son a job at the MTA, the Massachusetts Transportation Authority, which ran among other landmarks the old subway lines. When he proudly told Philip that he had planned his future, the son demurred and said he had other plans. He had been accepted by Ringling Brothers for Clown College. The old man laughed until his stomach ached, but then he realized that Philip was serious. "A clown? A clown? You went to MIT to be a clown?"

But Philip stayed strong and left that summer for Florida. His father never

38

talked to him again. Four months later, he received a certified letter from Foley, Hoag and Eliot informing him that he was officially and permanently disinherited from his father's considerable assets. That was it.

Philip finished the courses at the Clown College, learned even more magic tricks, and made a living from doing children parties or going on the road with the Ringling Brothers circus when there was a vacancy in the cast. He genuinely enjoyed the lights, the children, and the whole atmosphere of the hokey business. Then one day he had a call from his former instructor at the Clown College that they had received a letter from St. Jude's Hospital in Memphis, Tennessee which was looking for a permanent clown to help entertain the children, most of whom were cancer patients.

St. Jude had been started in 1962 by the old-time comedian Danny Thomas, and his daughter Marlo had vastly expanded its size and fund raising capacities. No family paid for medical care, food, lodging or transportation to the facility. It was totally free, and totally devoted to sick children. The hospital wanted a full time clown to help them plan activities for the children and their families on a day to day to basis. Philip accepted quickly and moved down to Tennessee.

After three years, he was immensely successful and had become as big a celebrity as the finest surgeon at St. Jude's. Then in 2000, the president of the United States honored St. Jude's work with the highest civilian award, the Medal of Freedom. The hospital decided to have Philip receive the award on behalf of the whole institution. The *Boston Globe* featured Philip on its front page, as a local boy made good who was to be honored by the nation's chief executive. When Philip's father saw the front page he was flushed with pride. He immediately sent his son in Tennessee $3,000 to buy the best suit he could find for that occasion. He used his connections with Senator Ted Kennedy to get tickets to the event in the White House, and he proudly but quietly showed up.

There the president was honoring important business and tech managers, movie stars, sports figures, leaders of the education reform movement, and also Philip. But Philip came in costume and stood out from the rest. The media loved the optic: the president with this smiling clown from St. Jude's. The president read a citation citing the clown's work and the mission of St. Jude, which was that "no child should die in the dawn of life." Audience members started crying at the sight, for children were what Americans liked to believe they were all about.

From his costume hung the bright gold medal on a red and white ribbon. And the president went out of his way to hug the clown, and to recite the hospital's 80% success record. That afternoon the president became the best fundraiser the hospital ever had. He apparently knew Danny Thomas from his days in show business, and told the audience an anecdote about meeting him on the stage of his television show, "Make Room for Daddy." He cited his Ohio roots, his long and distinguished career in all forms of media, but most of all his record as a philanthropist. As a young man, Thomas had promised St. Jude, the patron of hopeless causes, that he would build a hospital for children if he ever made it in show business, which no one thought he would. Later he kept his promise, and his daughter inherited his commitment. Philip was proud to stand there, and his father just stared at him from the fifth row of the room.

They never met. When Philip went back to Nashville, he gave the $3,000 to the fund for cardiac care for children, and his father was a major anonymous donor in his later years.

14. CRIME SCENE

In life there are two traits that come across as a poor mix: inexperience and self-assurance. I was a college president at only 41, and believed that those traits would never influence my behavior. But they did mix, to my chagrin and those of others. The campus was a tiny place; it overlooked the Sangre de Cristo mountains, an expression that meant, "blood of Christ," which the Spaniards believed they perceived on the hilltops at dusk. The land was full of rough scrubs and short greenery, but not the beautiful architecture or trees I was used to. From the president's office, I could see the mountains, the arroyos, and the dismal flatlands that marked the southwest.

I was sure I could make a difference in the lives and mores of the campus, and I was also certain that I could upend the traditions of laissez faire morality and flaccid humanism that we advertised to the students and their families. Everybody studied the same program each year. So all freshmen. for example. read Plato, Aristotle, and Aquinas, and the classes were so small that everyone knew each other, and they read together, ate together, and socialized together. That sort of community can be combustible. On the weekends one visited the same parties, and alcohol and sex were the only athletic competitions we had. Then on Monday, the rigor of the program kicked in and the students went in tandem back to work. I always thought the program was too hard even for adults, including the faculty pretentiously called "the tutors." I once said to the faculty, "Who the hell understands Hegel?"

One Tuesday morning I was approached by the dean of students with the information every president hates. There had been a rape on campus, a rape at one of those alcohol orgies. The campus surely had had those before, but usually the girls were pacified with a simple apology, and the guys were not sure what they had done under the influence.

But I was self-assured, and told the dean, "I will not tolerate that sort of behavior on a campus in my care. Find out the particulars and give them to the chief of police in Santa Fe." She was surprised, but did what she was instructed. I think she was startled that the new president would take the accusations seriously. Alcohol was the octane; rape was the outcome.

But I did take it seriously, and suspended the boy indefinitely, which meant he was missing whole segments of the great books. The board of trustees was not happy—that suspension was a reflection on the students, and it was against the high morality we advertised in our catalogue and were supposed to keep in our lives. The students were overwhelmingly pro-male and thought that anyone who went to these parties knew the game—necking, petting, groping, and then conquest. The girls were supposed to draw the line they wanted, and needed to be popular; the guys pushed the line and hoped to score that night. It was a simple index of behavior.

But I refused to go along. Finally after two weeks, I went to the county sheriff and said, "Sheriff, it has been two weeks since these charges were levied. I made the tough decision and now I am getting pounded by my board and by many students for having pushed this matter to you."

He looked at me, and solemnly remarked, "Look doc, I may be a country boy but even I know that in a city like Santa Fe I can't get a guilty plea when the girl was on top."

"Oh, I didn't know that."

"Yup, on top as naked as a jaybird. Sorry."

I went back to my office, ordered the boy re-instated. He never said anything to me. I never apologized for my error of judgment. And that day I learned some lessons about the mix of inexperience—my own—and self-confidence.

15. THE LAST RITES

I was sitting in my father's study, in his worn green leather chair, and looking out the bay window at the huge maple that covered one side of the backyard. In the summer it provided too much shade, and in the winter we worried that its boughs would fall off and into the house. One can never challenge the cycles of nature.

I had the Westlaw book on contract law on my lap, and grew tired of preparing for the final exam with its endless precedents and American briefs. Contract law was what most lawyers did for a living after all, so it was more important for nearly all of us than constitutional or international law. Ambition should be made of sterner stuff.

Finally realizing that I was totally distracted by the maple tree and bored in general by the law, I got up to walk down the hill of the lawn. The old man had originally bought a big lot that fronted on the edge of a state park. It was a good place for exercise and also for observing the natural array of animals and foliage. I walked over by the lake, deep in the woods. This was deer hunting season in New Jersey, and I could hear far away the sounds of rifle shots from guys who never even ate deer meat. Behind the trees were red signs warning hunters to be careful where they shot and to look closely in the directions where they were firing. I was walking without any rifle or even a fishing pole, just to see the startling array of nature.

I actually could see some hunters dressed in colorful garb not meant to scare the deer but to prevent their fellow hunters from firing at them. The irony of it all struck me, but deer season was deer season. We had to kill them or they would multiply out of control we were told by the state bureau of animal control. Thank God they did not run the maternity wards in the state hospitals.

Then I heard a fierce sound of agony, and looked up beyond the pack of evergreen trees and heard endless moaning, "God Almighty, they hit me. They hit me." I ran over to the sound, and there was a hunter sprawled out on the ground. He was wearing a L. L. Bean jacket, but with a Roman collar around his neck. I recognized quickly, he was the local Catholic priest from our own church. He was moaning. All I remembered was how I went to confession to him and he called my hot girlfriend an occasion of sin, which she indeed was. He saw me, grabbed my coat zipper and demanded, "Give me the last rites of the Church, and hear my confession."

"I am not a priest; I can't give you or anyone the last rites."

He got angry and then delirious, "Give me absolution of my sins, before it is too late. If you don't, I will die in a state of doubt." His cheek was bleeding profusely and I took his coat off and tried to make a tourniquet, but it was too big to stop the flow. I wasn't sure whether I should call 911 first or stop the bleeding which was gushing out. I ripped the sleeve off and used that to staunch the wound, but it was only partially effective. He cared little about the blood, "Give me absolution, I beg you. Don't let me die in despair. Give me absolution; I'll start, bless me for I have sinned."

I stood over him and listened as he repeated to me his sins, mortal and venal; I did not know that priests had such fantasies. I wondered if fantasies count as much as the real thing. Still I had no power to absolve him, but I listened, and when he was finished and fell into a sort of coma, I repeated, "God, forgive all his sins and grant him absolution according to your mercy." And I made the sign of the cross over him.

Then I shut up. I grabbed my cell phone and called the ambulance service which had been right near the deer park since they knew from previous years the perils from amateur hunters.

They came in quick time, and patched up his cheek to stop the blood. I breathed a sigh of relief.

"Did you stop that bleeding with that sleeve, son?"

"Yes, I did."

"Damn good job, he'll be ok, but will have a nasty scar there for quite a while, maybe permanently." The ambulance pulled out, crunching over the leaves, and left me alone with a bloody ripped jacket. I think I was a hero.

The next semester I finished up contract law, and came home. The old man insisted that I go to church, and there in the pulpit was the same pastor with a patch still on his cheek. For some reason he preached on and on, talking about death, "One never knows the time or place." He urged people to prepare for their Maker, for "it is rare that one can confess your sins in front of a priest at the very last moment. And even if you could, you may at the very last second have an impure thought or deny the existence of God. The devil comes like a thief in the night." The parishioners nodded, as if they all knew what he was talking about.

16. MY LEXUS

I began my college presidency in West Virginia on the Fourth of July 1989, and early in the morning I reverently took my three children across the border to Sharpsburg, Maryland, which is the site of the bloodiest battle of the Civil War, Antietam Creek. It was the single most costly conflict for both sides. And as we walked past the primitive church on the left side of the battlefield. I could see in my mind's eye, the pictures of Mathew Brady with the soldiers' bodies piled up like cord wood in front of the Spartan looking church. The kids didn't see that image in their minds. They never studied the Civil War.

That afternoon we all went to the Fourth of July town picnic at Morgan's Grove; I went for us to be seen for the first time. As I spun off the kids, who headed for the hot dogs and Kool-Aid, I made my way across the newly mowed field, and ended up talking quietly to an elderly woman dressed in a gingham dress with a flowered hat. She began, "Aren't you the new president at Shepherd College?"

"Yes, I am."

"And do you have any hobbies or interests besides work?"

"Yes, I enjoy baseball and writing."

"Which church do you belong to?"

"We actually just enrolled in St. Agnes yesterday."

"Isn't that a Catholic Church?"

"Yes, it is."

She turned on her heals and walked away. I did not realize I was the first Roman Catholic to be president in the 100 years history of the college.

As I looked around, I noticed there was not a single black person at the picnic. The region, called the Eastern Panhandle, was the only area in West Virginia that was viciously anti-Lincoln during the Civil War. Not to be outdone, the Great Emancipator sent in Union troops to guarantee the loyalty of those counties. There were people who never had forgotten his actions, and passed down their views to their progeny about how grandpappy had lost his wealth, which I sarcastically said was human beings, slaves.

Behind a gracious older lady, was James Earl Turner, a 6'4" well-built All American who had played basketball for Gale Catlett at WVU. Catlett was a state wide celebrity and was even thinking of running for the Senate against the venerable Robert C. Byrd. Turner was the golden boy of the panhandle, and was president of the best bank in the county, the Eastern Panhandle National Bank, which overshadowed all the rest in West Virginia.

"You the new president? I have been waiting for you."

"Well, I just started Friday, but you are on my list to see."

"How about tomorrow morning? Or don't you academics get up early in the morning? How about 9 o'clock?

"How about 8 a.m.?"

"Sounds good, you know where I am?"

"Yup, l will be glad to see you at 8 sharp!"

Then he moved gracefully away and other lesser mortals came up to me.

The next morning I wore my best money-raising suit and arrived a bit ahead of time.

"Well, you got up. Good for you." Bluntly he began, "What would you like me to do for you in your honeymoon period?"

"I want to talk to you about heading up a group of bankers and businessmen to raise scholarship money. Our fees are low, but so is the per capita income in West Virginia."

"I have no problem contributing a modest amount, but I don't know if I want to head up a group and be that associated with a guy I don't even know."

"Fair enough, wait and see what you like," I responded.

"Also, I don't care for the college—its administration is weak and has been poorly run for years. Lazy faculty who teach nine hours a week, *a week*, who spend a good deal of their time trying to get into the underpants of teenage co-eds, and guys who never come to a basketball game even when my son plays."

I was a bit annoyed at his abrupt idea of West Virginia hospitality.

"Look, let's just forget it."

"No, no, I and my wife Lorelei Belle noticed that the Board of Trustees has never given you a welcome party to the community. They have no real class, we'd like to give you a large party where you can meet everyone in one night. Besides we are proud of our renovated house off Main Street. It used to be an old YMCA and Lorelei Belle had done marvelous things inside. You will enjoy it, and we all will give you more advice on how to run that college of yours. I am sure you'll appreciate it! But we are the elders of this community, you know."

"That will be nice, Jim."

So a month later my wife and I arrived at the remodeled structure and entered the fascinating rehabilitation. The main element of the structure was the massive old gymnasium changed into a classical ballroom. The tables were filled with food, and throngs of people arrived in expensive suits and long dresses that smelled of cash and carry. We walked in and Lorelei came up dressed in an Oleg Cassini dress and Prada accessories. She was tall, thin, breastless, and with a charming but haughty manner. We stayed for three hours listening to old stories, ancient grievances against the college, and the cool attitude of my predecessor. Late into the night, in ambled U.S. Senator Robert C. Byrd, to the delight of the crowd. He walked directly over to me, and said sarcastically, "Ah, I really don't care for the current president we have in the White House, so I will make you my favorite president! Come here Mr.

President, I want to put a NASA installation in Shepherdstown and you are central to my dream."

"Yes, sir, will do."

So the days ticked away and by Christmas I saw the headlines in a local newspaper announcing, "Eastern Panhandle National Bank closed by FDIC and state insurance commission." Apparently, the agencies were in over the weekend and closed the whole bank down. Turner was out, no one could find him.

A week of confusion was settled when the chairman of the board, Amos Gifford, a patrician and graduate of Brown University, came to see me. He looked like Walter Pidgeon in the old movies and talked the same way. I glanced aimlessly out the president's office windows as he came and parked his beautiful black Lexus in my spot. Amos walked in and quietly knocked on the door, "May I come in, Mr. President?"

"Of course, any member of the State Commission on Higher Education is always welcome."

"I come here on behalf of another board, the Eastern Panhandle National Bank Board, which has decided to ask you to take over the presidency of the institution. We need your prestige and influence to repair the damage Jim left. We will pay you four times what you are making here and of course immediately lease a car."

I was totally shocked, "What happened to Turner?"

"Let's just say he was lousy manager. Knew how to run everybody's business but ours. You must have noticed that."

I said little and thanked Amos. He properly rose up and asked me when he would hear from me.

"I appreciate the confidence, but I am not a bank manager, I'm an educator. I can't see how I can change. Thank you though."

"Well at least you know how to make a decision, unlike your predecessor. Thank you for being so honest."

Amos marched out toward his beautiful black Lexus, and he drove out of my space. Why does black and rich look so, well, rich? All I could say to myself was, "Also, a new Lexus, What a car! Good choice, Amos."

17. IN FRANCE

After four years I graduated from Swarthmore College with both academic honors and a fine record playing varsity lacrosse. I majored in French literature and did a senior thesis on Andre Gide's *L'Immoraliste*. But when my last year came I realized that I had no job prospects, which I would have had had I studied Mandarin or Spanish. I went to the college placement office and leafed through the lists of openings and came upon an interesting memorandum sent to select schools from the French Embassy. It announced that the Ministry of Education wanted to hire six French-speaking Europeans or Americans to teach in the smaller cities in elementary grades so its students could come in contact with foreigners who respected their traditions. I jotted down the address of the ministry and sent them my resume and a chapter of my work on Gide. In two weeks I heard back from the vice minister in Washington, asking me if I would be interested in a two year contract to teach in the village of Lisieux. A small apartment was provided with a modest stipend. The opportunity excited my sense of adventure, and so I accepted.

Three months later I was on Air France to Charles de Gaulle airport, and from there the Ministry of Education arranged for bus transportation to Lisieux, in the Normandy area. The reception I received from the townspeople was truly moving, and I was proudly shown both their cathedral and the public school I would be working in. The apartment was small, meticulously clean, kept in shape by a dedicated landlady.

The first months of teaching were actually refreshing. As an American, I was a bit of an oddity for the nine-year-old children in my class, but they loved my accent and also my teaching them their language and reciting the stories of old France and its famed heroes. At noon time, the students went outside with the other classes, and played soccer, tag, or ran around to get their energy level down for the afternoon classes. My children were especially active, and I noticed one girl, Therese, who did not participate much in organized sports, but spent her lunch hour gathering flowers which she put in a vase in the classroom each afternoon. She was a kind and gentle soul. When we had a new student arrive, especially from Algeria or from other former French colonies, she went out of her way to introduce the student to the others and find a way for the newcomer to enter into play in the yard, and then was also especially kind in the class. Some students had a difficult time with academic French, so I would often tutor after class and offer them personal instruction. Therese would stay to give them moral support and then walk them home.

Being an American bachelor, I received many invitations to dinner from the town folk. Sometimes they just wanted to talk about America and recall the heroism of the Yanks at Normandy so many years ago. But often the mothers introduced me to their attractive daughters or nieces who were older teenagers with narrow figures, long inviting legs, and beautiful smiles. They often looked like local models for Paris designers. I invited some of them on dates, but mainly they wanted to talk about topics like existentialism or phenomenology which was not exactly what I had in mind.

Therese's parents invited me to dinner one Saturday afternoon. They had a large family of girls, and they were all deeply religious. They were especially proud of the two oldest girls who were entering the Carmelite order, a group of reclusive nuns who prayed in sealed off convents for the souls in purgatory. After a superb dinner, they stopped and prayed the rosary to the Virgin Mary. It was their routine which I did not join in but simply respected.

One day I saw a very sad Therese enter class. She had learned from her father that the French government was making an exception so as to execute a convict named Poutine, who had murdered a pregnant mother and two little children with an ax in a home invasion that seemed to have no purpose at all. The government had decided that he deserved the death penalty, and he was to be executed at end of the month.

She had just heard about the penalty and that he would die by his own request without the last rites; nobody from the French Church said anything. She told me she was going to devote herself to a novena of nine days of prayers for his final conversion. I did not agree or disagree, but noticed that from time to time in class she seemed preoccupied, and then she would almost jerk herself back to the happenings of class. Finally on the day of his decided death, she asked me if they had carried it out. I told her, "The newspaper said that he walked by the priest on the platform toward the hangman's noose, spat at the clergyman, then stopped and suddenly he kissed the feet of the crucifix that the priest was carrying." To Therese, God had answered her request, as she told me He had so often in her past. The killer's final moment had been reconciliation with God.

She was an extraordinary child, one you could love easily. But after one year at Lisieux, I resigned my position unexpectedly. I realized that I could not live in Therese's world, and yet I could not live outside it. And so I fled.

18. LOST CHILD (in verse)

My paternal grandfather,
Whom I was respectfully named after,
Came to this land of opportunities and dreams
Back in 1911, right before
Congress enacted in a fit of anger
The severest restrictions on Italians entering.
We used to say it was not a coincidence!
They were invited but not welcomed.
He lived in Orange, New Jersey
When Orange was a livable place for families.
Down the street around the sharp corner,
Near the large Ballantine billboard,
Was the church of Our Lady of Mt. Carmel,
One of the most beloved saints in Italy.
The church was maintained by the Capuchins,
Poor shadows of the disciples of St. Francis.
They knew everyone, good or bad,
Or like most men indifferent.
Grandma went to Mass every morning,
Grandpa when reminded of God's blessings,
Said, "C'esta," if He exists.
He observed that he never
Saw a thin monk.

Grandpa wore the work ethic lightly,
His father had been mayor in San Polino,
And retired at age 35,
Sitting till sunset in the piazza
Drinking red wine and watching the girls.

Grandpa left with seven cousins
To explore the new world in a most leisurely way.
He was once a collector from Italian grocers
Of the money from pasta sales,

But his friends needed funds to survive,
It was the 1920s,
Even worse was coming.
So he loaned them money
Which he could not pay to Ronzoni.
The company threaten to arrest him,
But the family worked out repayment.
Then he went to West Orange,
And became a time keeper
For the Thomas Alva Edison company,
And saw from the catwalk
The old graying genius taking
Constant catnaps, which Grandpa envied.

He and his paesani formed a club.
In the darkness of Orange,
They gossiped like old women,
Played cards and bocce,
And drank wine they made
In the midst of Prohibition,
Which was a WASP preoccupation then.
Babes in Italy drank wine not polluted water.

He would go to the club every night,
While Grandma sewed powder puffs.
One day, she had to go out
And asked Grandpa to watch
The youngest boy, a six-year-old,
Sure, said Grandpa
And he took him to the club,
Where the boy watched them play cards all night,
Drink wine, and he eventually curled up
Asleep in the dark corner.

At the end of a longer than usual night,
They all left the club
With its covered windows.
Grandpa slowly walked back to the house,
Grandma was in the kitchen still working,
He just sat on his old rocker,
And read the day's *Il Progresso,*
The neo-Fascist rag owned by the Pope family
Who mass produced lousy tomato sauce.

Grandma finished in the kitchen,
"Come Ponzione, time to get to bed."

But he wasn't around.
"Michele, where is the boy?"
Good God, Grandpa had left his son at the club.
In anger, then in panic, she screamed
To high heaven at Grandpa
Who seemed at first just confused.

Meanwhile, back at the street
Across from the Gothic church
The little boy stood crying
In front of the closed club.
He had climbed out the front window,
Which was covered with a robust picture
Of the great liberator, Garibaldi.
He cried out, "Papa, papa."
Then suddenly up the street waddled,
A bulky monk on a nightly walk,
Who stopped to talk to the boy.
No, he did not know his own address,
"Over that street, over there, I think."
But the monk took him by the hand,
He knew the neighborhood well,
And went to three or four doors—
People greeted him happily, and
One old lady said, "He is Ponzione,
Vivizenza's boy.
She lives on Duane Street
In the third house with the statue of
The Sacred Heart near the door, padre."

He walked up the dark alley
Onto the little lawn
Up the wooden creaking stairs,
And rang the bell.
A panicky mother was on her way out.
There was her boy in the hands of a monk,
"Maybe, you are back.
Like the prodigal son," the monk smiled.
She quickly invited the monk in,
But they had not had dinner to share,
For she had little to offer even the family
And made a soup of ketchup and spices.
But Grandpa in a fit of embarrassment,
Offered the monk wine, glass after glass.

The monk drank a few easily,

And said, "I must leave now
I came out for a short walk
And ended up on a happy venture!"
Grandma was so grateful,
She looked out at the dark,
And searched for a candle for the monk
To lead him back to the rectory.

She first asked him to bless
The ramshackle house,
Not for the evil in it,
But just for the misfortunes.
As he stepped out on the dark porch,
She reverently lit the candle,
Gave it to the monk.
He moved on toward the church,
And the dark comprehended it not.

The next morning,
Grandma went to the very early Mass,
To thank the Blessed Mother,
For she too had lost her child once,
Or so it said in the Gospel of Luke.
And as she knelt down later at her statue,
She felt the monk lightly tap on her shoulder,
"Have a candle, blessed by Bishop O'Connor."

Once home, Grandma put it on the empty table
In the lonely dining room
In front of the picture of the Infant of Prague,
Who seemed to shine even in the fog.

19. INHERITANCE

Steve O'Toole was a freshman at Lehigh University, class of 2001, and knew he did not belong there. As his father graciously said once, "You're not college material." But his grandfather, whom he was named after, was a billionaire who had made his money as an engineer who had invented one of the transistors produced at Bell Labs at Murray Hill. He was also co-winner of the Nobel Prize, and a graduate of Lehigh to which he gave generously. So Steve ended up in Lehigh, but grandpa candidly told him engineering was not his game, so he majored in business, a not uncommon field of study for the rich and dull.

As Christmas approached, grandpa suffered a massive heart attack and died in his easy chair wondering how his work could be used to solve the riddle of cancer, not an easy connection. Steve briefly mourned the death but had no plans to attend the funeral. The next day he received a phone call from the family lawyer: he had to come to the family meeting the very next day. It was extremely important, he insisted. So Steve did as he was told, and arrived to the surprise of the family. The lawyer droned on listing the beneficiaries—a million for his son, two million for grandpa's girlfriend, a million here and there to respected charities. And then the lawyer took a long breath, "And to Steve, I leave $125 million." The participants gasped. No one in the family went over to congratulate him. Steve was a bit distracted at first, but then repeated, "Wow, $125 million."

He shook the lawyer's hand and walked out to the building's elegant Deco entrance on Lexington Avenue. All of a sudden, it did not really seem so cold. He ran to Penn Station and took the Amtrak back to Pennsylvania all the way to old Lehigh. Except for the liquor-charged parties and bad football, he really did not care for the place. Somewhat haphazardly he packed his possessions, and headed back to Greenwich Village to look for an apartment. Who the hell wanted to stay in Bethlehem, Pennsylvania? He did not need to cart most of his stuff, he could buy what he needed in the city; boy, it was great to be rich.

He walked around the wide streets and the Washington Square area, carrying a certified check in his right pocket for $125 million. He deposited the whole thing in the nearby Bank of America. Now what was he going to do with his life? At 22 he was a very rich, young man. It felt great.

But he wanted some guidance, not just on taxes but what is the purpose of life. For a week or so he sat quietly on a bench in Washington Square, watching disheveled men throwing bread crumbs to filthy pigeons. One cool afternoon, he noticed a used catalogue on his bench—evening courses at nearby NYU. He aimlessly paged through it and came across a group of courses "life actualization," and the name of a course on comparative religions with the title, "Learn the Meaning of Life."

It was a noncredit course, taught by Robert Thurman, a famed Buddhist scholar who was a professor uptown at Columbia University. Steve was interested immediately, since he had always been fascinated by Buddha who was originally a prince. He was wealthy, beloved, and sealed off by his royal parents from the sadness of the world: sickness, poverty, pain, death—and then one day he escaped his keepers and was overwhelmed by what he saw. He spent his whole life trying to help people cope with their vicissitudes. Many of his followers sought to reach his final step of enlightenment, though prayer, mediation and a denial of the ailments of the world. But Steve didn't realize what all that meant in everyday life. He enrolled—most of the kids in the course had prayer wheels, and in the room was a golden statue of Padmasambhava, the master of Tartaric Buddhism from Tibet.

Thurman was a convincing and dedicated speaker, and some soon learned that his daughter was the beautiful actress Uma Thurman, the very equivalent of a "10" on any man's scale. Thank God, Robert had renounced celibacy.

Steve was attentive to Buddhism as the course went on. But after ten weeks he was not sure it was for him. He loved the world, like all rich men do, and enjoyed its favors. He did not approach enlightenment, even at the lower levels, and he talked one night to Thurman, who listened and listened and stressed the importance of patience and the allures to avoid. This was very hard in New York City. It was Babylon itself, Thurman insisted, and then he took a limo home to the affluent Morningside Heights, near Columbia.

A few days later, Steve was going to Penn Station, to visit his girlfriend back at Lehigh. She wasn't Uma but she was dependable, so to speak. Returning to New York City, he got out of a cab, and ended up in front of a tiny Catholic chapel where many actors went to Mass rather than the garish St. Patrick's on 5th Avenue. Steve just stared at it; despite his last name—O'Toole—grandpa hated the Catholic Church, saying it was a corrupt collection of lazy priests who dealt in mumbo jumbo. He never gave religion much thought until it was too late, for making money and inventing innovations took all of his time.

For some reason, Steve went inside and saw there in the front pew a Capuchin with his habit covering most of the nearby space, saying a rosary. He was from the Franciscan Order and had the look of a monk who had been around, and smelled of candles and sanctity. Steve went up to him and asked how he could learn more about the Catholic faith. The old man looked up and smiled as if he had waited for this call his entire vocation.

They talked a bit, and the monk and Steve were to meet six more times. Steve had no problem with major points of contention: the papacy, the Virgin Mary, the practice of confession, and the old dispute, indulgences. But Steve did have a strong objection with the notion that bread and wine became the body and blood of Christ in real terms. He could accept them as symbolic or a special substances, but he could not accept or understand why it was necessary to believe in transubstantiation. The old monk explained it was the very center of Catholicism, and Steve listened respectfully. Finally he decided he could get some sense of direction, for Catholicism had a lot of answers to questions that had bothered him.

He was ready to convert, confess his sins, and receive the host soon. He appeared this one Sunday and the chapel was filled to the limits. For it was Palm Sunday, one of the high holy days of his new faith. As people lined up to receive communion, he deferred to the regulars and ended up at the very end of the line. When he came up to receive his first communion, the priest embarrassingly looked directly at him, "I'm sorry, I have no more hosts, that has never happened before."

"What do you mean no hosts?"

"I guess we never expected this crowd, especially at the last Mass of the day. I am most sorry, my son."

So Steve left the chapel, and walked down 33rd street. He looked at the lights on Madison Square Garden, stepped over the homeless, bought a copy of the *New York Post*, and wondered if what happened was some sign. He had tried Buddhism and now Catholicism, and yet he still wondered what his purpose in life was. Perhaps he was just a true grandson of his grandfather and inherited not just his money, but his attitudes.

20. PARROTS IN PARADISE

(for Maria S.)

Grandpa was sitting at the head of the table, a nominal honor for the dinner the aunts put together for the weekend of Our Lady of Mount Carmel. That feast day was celebrated especially in July by Neapolitan families who emigrated to the United States. It was followed by a parade, a Mass, fireworks, and entertainment booths that occupied the church's parking lot. The family, as long as any remembered, was in charge of the Mount Carmel banner, a blue satin picture of the Virgin surrounded by gold fringes. As it began to get worn, the matrons of the family refused the very generous offer of the Madison Historical Society to place it under glass to preserve it.

Grandpa was rather quiet that day, thinking of better times with Mama, and when these adults were his young children. On the table was the usual: baked ziti, chicken parmesan, meatballs and sausage, salads, crispy bread, and assorted displays of desserts. It was a family of diabetics who loved starches and sweets. Luckily though, Grandpa had to say nothing, for his oldest child, whom he called Salvatore, and the others called "Sadie," was explaining his latest findings on the family genealogy. He had traced back the roots of the clan to the eighteenth century, and even found that one had married a Ben Franklin, whatever that meant. But today, he was explaining that the family just didn't end up on the east coast of the United States, but had gone to Australia, Canada, Argentina, and even nearby Cuba. He was proposing that the family send ambassadors to each family branch and then report back. For some reason, the idea caught on like wildfire, especially when he told the diners that Grandma's family, the Perones, was related to the Argentine dictator, Juan Peron, the husband of the elegant Evita.

He felt that Grandpa should go to Cuba to represent the family; but Grandpa rarely went out of New Jersey or nearby New York City, so he was very hesitant, but when everybody seemed enthusiastic about the other areas, he consented. He was going to Cuba.

Cuba in those days was ruled by a corrupt dictatorship that invited in the Mafia to run its new casinos. It was a dirty marriage of convenience. But Grandpa did not know that, and instead concentrated on writing to the Cuban branch inviting himself as coming on behalf of the family. His letter was immediately answered in Italian, so he knew they had more memories than his own children of the language and culture.

When he arrived, he was greeted at the Havana Airport by a huge crowd of people who hailed him as if he were a celebrity. They hugged and kissed him, took his decrepit luggage, and grabbed him by the arm to their cars. He was surprised that they spoke not only Spanish but also Italian and English, and he had no problem understanding his fellow countrymen.

At home, they took him to the best room in what was a hacienda, and then insisted on introducing him to every member of the household, and to the extended cousins who drove from Havana to pay their respects. It was a long, elegant house with a huge sunroom that had in the midst of it a caged parrot. Grandpa had only once before seen a parrot, and that was in Naples when the bird, perched on the shoulder of the great clown Puccinella, did a routine with the comic. This parrot was apparently the special pet of a little girl of six or so with big beautiful brown eyes and a quick smile. The parrot was less impressed, and kept on calling the old man, "Tonto" which meant idiot.

Night after night they would have splendid dinners, a mix of Cuban food and traditional Italian fare. During the days, the kids went to school, for their parents wanted them to make something of themselves, and the parents went to work. He was a doctor, and she was a manager of a hotel nearby, so Grandpa often ended up alone in the beautiful house. One day the doctor took him to see the town plaza with the stunning church dedicated to the patron saint of Cuba, St. Lazarus, the friend of Jesus who was raised from the dead and later became a bishop of the new faith. It was a magnificent structure built from hard rock and was imbedded with jewels inside the rocks. In the church was a statue of Lazarus, and on a side altar a statue of their other patron, Saint Barbara, who was wrapped in a red sheet, her color. Grandpa had never heard of either of them, but the Cubans effortlessly mixed the Yoruba customs with the traditional Roman Latin rite. So much seemed strange. There was though much more singing and even dancing at the Masses, very different from St. Vincent Martyr in New Jersey where most of the old people fingered their rosaries while the priest mumbled along.

One day, the old man went to church by himself and saw a fairly young American dressed only in cut off fatigues and Marine Corps boots. He was planting flowers around the whole church, an activity that Grandpa was no stranger to. He went up to him and praised his choice of plants, and then inquired where he was from. "Minnesota, but via the Marine Corps in Korea."

Apparently, this well-built man had finished his service in the war years ago, but was still affected by its horrors. To remind him of the beauty of life, he planted flowers wherever he went. He was in Cuba with a buddy in the Corps who invited him to join his rich family outside Havana. He came and began to plant flowers at the house, and then asked permission to start a flower garden around the church. Grandpa also instinctively dropped down, and helped him plant.

The veteran was reciting a well-known Cuban poem by Nicholas Guillen:

When I see and touch

Myself, Juan with Nothing more yesterday
And today Juan with Everything,
And yet today,
I turn my eyes, I look,
I see and touch
And wonder how it could be.

The young man told Grandpa the stories of his terrible times at Seoul, Inchon, and Pusan. He hated the war they drafted him for, and saw no glory in killing, or in the mud trenches where one rarely saw beauty of any type. He kept on he said by the memories of flowers back home, and of spring times when the sun kissed the land and implanted flowers and trees.

After a week, he just vanished. Grandpa heard that he had just gone back to the States.

But Grandpa kept the gardens rich, and visited the church to pray to saints he never heard of. Then one day he came back to the doctor's house, and he gave the parrot several seeds, nuts and pieces of fruit, which the parrot loved. He began calling grandpa "Tio" and was spouting about the need to find the "tesoro." Grandpa did not know what he was babbling about, until little Maria told him that he was constantly talking about a tesoro or treasure buried near the old cemetery. The next afternoon, Grandpa went into the sunroom, dropped more seeds and nuts, but held up the fruit chips. "Where, parrot, is the tesoro? Where near the cementerio?"

The nasty bird called him a "tonto," fool, again, and then said out of nowhere, "Tonto, under the biggest tree."

Grandpa dropped the fruit, ran for a shovel, and went to the cemetery, and there far away was a huge tree with a big hump at its base. He absentmindedly started shoveling and after a foot and a half of dirt he found a rusty box. Grandpa pulled the handle, and it was so old it just came off in his hand. He shoveled around the box, and pulled the whole thing up. Inside were sacks of old Spanish gold pieces, worth a small fortune even back then.

Grandpa recovered the box, and wondered what type of bags he needed to carry them. He had come all the way to Cuba to become rich! That night though some rebels burnt the church of Saint Lazarus and the whole steeple with the cross of dying Jesus was consumed. The community was devastated and the pastor, an old Capuchin, told the people that they did not have the money in the parish to fix it. It would be best to close their old church.

Grandpa heard the wailing and crying that day at Mass, and he felt guilty. God had not made him to be a rich man; he knew that in his heart. So he talked to the Capuchin and took him to the old tree, and said that there was enough gold to fix the church and even build a school for the young where they could learn their letters and also their faith. The priest called it a good deed in a naughty world.

The next Sunday, the Capuchin informed the people that a prophet from a foreign land had given him the money to fix the church and to build a school as well. The faithful prayed before the statue of St. Barbara, and Grandpa just watched silently.

He had to get home after three weeks, and he was leaving the next day. As he said goodbye to his new family, he stopped by the parrot's cage, and said "Adios." The patriot looked at him cross eyed, and responded, "Tio Tonto," Uncle Fool.

21. THE BOYS OF WINTER

(for Patrick)

Sometimes birthdays do not come on birthdays, and such happened to me in the brisk autumn of 2016. My son Patrick had decided to take me to the new Yankee Stadium to see my home team play. It was a fine day for baseball, and the field has that special shade of green that seems more graphic as it jumps out at you. It is still America in a more idyllic period when it was possible if not desirable to ignore time, and in which boys and men can play a game without quarters, without periods, without time clocks. Baseball is like life itself; we know when it begins, but never when it ends, and so experts keep needless records since the nineteenth century on hits, runs, errors, and the conduct of the teams' line up of players.

Usually I sit in the cheaper mezzanine seats, for the prices have gone up so substantially. It costs $200 today to take your child to a major league game, and the best seats are usually held all season by corporations, filled with sharp-eyed lawyers and out-of-shape hedge fund managers—the same types of guys who show up at Sotheby's and Christie's to buy art not for the beauty of it, but as an investment.

But my son likes to live first class, so he bought tickets in the special glass boxes overlooking the field, with seats outside, and inside was food, drink, and sociability that one can't get in rows of seats in section 206. Our collection of seats and the boxes were labeled simply #5 after the great DiMaggio. Inside I grabbed a rubbery hot dog and a coke and went outside to see the game in all its traditional glory. But there were very few of us in the seats of #5. I asked Pat what was going on. He knew that the Yanks had hired retired baseball stars to parade from one suite to another and sign autographs. I went back in and saw the great Mets pitcher Doc Gooden was coming our way.

For some reason I recognized him down the hall in another suite. He was a tall, thin black man in a gym suit and sneakers, and a great smile on his face. It was the Doc, the premier pitcher of the 1980s, who in 1985 was the Cy Young winner. My son knew more about him than I, for he was a rabid Mets fan in part because of my lethargy. I preferred to take him in those days from north Jersey to the safe middle class neighborhood of Shea Stadium in Queens rather than the rough cowboy environment of knives and broken bottles of the South Bronx where the House that Ruth Built was now lying. So he committed the ultimate act of treason, changing allegiances from the greatest championship athletic team in history to an expansion team with aging ballplayers and anemic results. As Mets manager, Casey Stengel, once said, "Does anybody here know how to play this game?"

One day I took him to the old Shea Stadium on a lark, and we had no tickets. I was determined not to let him down and was willing to pay scalpers' prices. But we got two boxes on the left side of home plate and behind the protective mesh. The game was about to start, and the scalper wanted to unload the tickets and did so at face value. And that was the first time I saw play Doc Gooden who was then pitching for the Mets and was at the height of his powers. It was July 1986, and I watched him intently. I realized that as close as we were, I really could barely see the ball as it whizzed by the batters. Neither could they.

That was 1986, and now it was two decades later, and I watched as a quick, snaky line filed in as he sat quietly at the end of the suite, up on a high armless chair, eating a hot dog quickly and signing all sorts of objects with his other hand. We had nothing, and so I had Pat stand in line while I hustled out and bought a baseball. Typical of pro baseball teams, the ball was double the cost of the usual Rawling ball. I paid the price and philosophically made my way back to the line. Patrick was in the middle, but the line was creeping along. I left him and went behind Gooden and talked to his daughter who was his agent in a sense. She told me that he now worked with kids in rehab and also gave inspirational speeches to companies. For years he had been plagued by bouts of cocaine addiction which surely shortened his career on the mound.

Our line moved very slowly in part because Doc took each ball and carried on a conversation with each patron. Finally it was our turn.

I said "We saw you at Shea and it was the finest performance I have ever seen."

Pat intruded, "Yeh, we saw you in July 1986, the year of the World Series."

"*Who the hell remembered that?*," I thought. Well he and Doc did.

Then Gooden stopped and told my son, "You know who taught me about pitching? My daddy, we used to play on the farm near the old barn till dusk came." He smiled and fondly remembered better days, warmer afternoons, and seasons of hope. He handed back the signed ball and we thanked him.

Doc smiled again. Following us was a father with his son who was a bit mentally challenged, and his father proudly told Doc how his kid was going to be a pitcher also. Doc stopped, pulled the boy over to him, and explained that to throw a curve ball you not only needed to snap the wrist, but also pull the movement through the whole upper arm. I never knew that. The kid was grateful for the personal attention, and tried it a bit after he received an autographed ball.

I gave my son our ball, but I have the memory of a truly great man stopping to teach the young and not so gifted. He was still in some ways a superstar just as in 1985, but some days old age and drug abuse came upon him. Then two weeks later, I picked up a copy of the *New York Post* in which Doc's great friend Darryl Strawberry was angry because he missed a joint appearance. He insisted that Doc was an addict again, and he went public he said to save his friend.

I wondered to myself if the "outing" would have any effect, or if in fact it simply deprived him of the only job he had in his retirement. The *Post* carried the story for two days, and then it went on to another scandal.

Sometimes, as I watch the game, even in the minors, even Little League teams, I wonder if it would have been better to mind one's own business in life. Let him play out his life his way as he wished. Still in the green grass, in the summer of our lives, baseball is too precious to be sullied. Even at my age you can be disillusioned.

Say, it ain't so, Doc, say it ain't so. Be the guy I remember in 1986, the guy I just saw teaching the young the tricks of the old heroes.

22. DEATH COMES HOME

The most pernicious problem I faced as a college president was the pervasiveness of alcohol abuse. I had banned alcohol totally on campus, but the college was surrounded by liquor stores, bars, and fraternities that did not care about my dictum. When I was asked about tailgate parties at football games, I said "no," and was greeted one day by the huge linebacker, Sam Huff of the Giants, who represented the beer interests in West Virginia. Up into my face, he wanted to know why I was opposed to tailgating parties, and luckily the host stepped in and said, "Sam, he is just doing his job." I said later that I felt like knocking him on his fat ass, but when someone asked me why I didn't do that, I responded, "Because he would have killed me." They had obviously never seen the CBS TV film, "The Violent World of Sam Huff."

Still I stood firm.

Seeing a pickup truck one Friday carrying a keg of beer, I followed it to the fraternity house it was meant for. Outside my jurisdiction.

Then one night, death came home. Two cars full of students were playing chicken off campus, after a long period of bar hopping. The result was a massive car crash, two boys killed, and several in the hospital.

The campus was split based on the friendships of the dead boys. One was a fine football player, and there was a feeling among the other boy's family that the college somehow favored him in his death. The first boy was buried in a Methodist service, and the young woman preached a sermon which instead of remembering the boy criticized the campus administration for not doing enough about illegal drinking. Three times we had reported the bars to the ABC for selling to minors, and nothing resulted. Later I got a letter from one of the people at the Methodist services saying, "The minister was out of place." I just responded saying, "Tempers were high during this tragedy involving the very young."

The second boy was a Catholic, and was buried according to its ancient rites. I went to that funeral too, and was startled to hear from people later that my athletic director told people that he expected I would go to the Catholic service but not the Methodist one, since I was a Catholic. That remark made me furious, so I called him in. He was an out of shape, foul mouth assistant football coach with rotten teeth, whose favorite word in the august English language was f_ck, as a verb, a noun, a gerund, an adjective, a participle and whatever else the conversation needed.

Once I had to tell him that the neighbors who were devout black Baptists complained about the language on the football practice field. He said he would "talk to the boys." I told him, "They are talking about you."

Then I moved in as I rarely did, "Your wife is quoted as saying that you remarked that you did not expect me as a Catholic to come to a Methodist service. Did you say such a stupid thing?"

"No, no, you know how much I respect you and your position. It was my wife not me." It was so obviously a cowardly lie. Then I did what I never do, I went into my male Jersey macho voice, "Boy, you better get control of your family."

It was a bit sexist for me, but I really enjoyed it.

Soon after, another girl went to a frat party. Girls go because they want to be popular, even with the low lives on campus. She drank so much so quickly that she died of alcohol poisoning. The students planted a nice plaque in the lawn in front of her high rise dormitory, but no one said "Let's make sure this doesn't happen again."

After I left the college, tailgating parties came back in. At one game, near a black pickup with the tailgate down, a drunken father was consuming the hard stuff and, for some reason that is now forgotten, he got angry at his two boys, who were students at the college, and shot both of them dead.

The college had also reversed my tightly administered ban on guns on campus because it was huntin' season.

23. THE RAILING

Santa Fe is the only state capital in the nation with no airport. One has to go into smoggy Albuquerque and then take a rarely air-conditioned mini-bus through the lands of the Pueblo reservations some sixty miles to that ancient city. I had to go to Albuquerque to finalize my formal arrangements and to get approval for the two other scholars I was bringing in. I am a physicist and was inviting a well-known engineer from Cal Tech and a particle physicist from Berkley to join me. We were all being well paid, at least well enough to put up with the bus moving slowly from the new airport to the oldest city. We were to examine what could only be called an anomaly.

It was scorching hot, but the air-conditioned bus barely acknowledged the temperature. I sat on the right side to avoid the Southwest sun, and next to me came a buxom, tanned blonde in an inviting sundress whose hem was two inches higher than normal. She was young enough to entice, but old enough to know better. I smiled at her and as we began she put her white sunhat on the top shelf. The bus tour was $25 each way—in cash. She only had tens, but I helped her break a bill. All I could imagine looking at her was that she would be a great lay if I could get the chance.

She was going to The Hotel at the end of the old Santa Fe Trail for a conference of Associated Press executives, important since the UPI had been dissolved. But she had forgotten to make a reservation, so she would just arrive and hope they had a vacancy. Frankly it was an old, moldy, bug ridden place, and if I had had approval, I would have stayed at the new Sheraton. For some reason, I told her I had a room with two single beds and she was welcome to stay with me. Could fortune be so good? Before she responded, I gave her my key and said nonchalantly that I would be in late, so please leave the door open. Without a moment of protest, she thanked me, and we both got off at the last stop. Her smile lit up the dusty road, and she moved gracefully toward the hotel, and I looked scientifically at her back form.

We walked down the next street in the center of the city square. Old Indian women were selling their wares; my favorite was little statues called the "storytellers," mothers with children sitting all over them as they apparently told tales of lore. I was a sucker for memorabilia. Three blocks away was the Loretto Church which my team had been hired to examine inside.

We were to give to the Archdiocese a final verdict on the famed wooden rail that reached up to the top of their 22-foot-high apex. Apparently, the original architects forgot to plan for a stair case to the choir loft, and the nuns were left with no way to get up to the top. So they decided on a spiral staircase. No one could figure out how the wooden railing and staircase with no iron nails, no wooden pieces, no properly sized stairs all fit together. Yet it just hung there from top to bottom perfectly. So my colleagues and I were called in—the best and the brightest Archbishop Sanchez called us—to explain this weird phenomenon. People would come from all over the world and say a prayer. Even Pope John Paul II was going to skip Houston on his next trip and visit the modest church, for he was a common follower of the folk Catholicism that he grew up knowing in Krakow.

We were to lend the authority of science to the whole debate, so as not to embarrass the Church. Since Galileo they had learned not to take on the power of science. Almost on time, the three of us showed up in front of the tiny chapel. John Wildenbloom of Berkeley carried a large suitcase full of engineering instruments; Peter McNeil of Caltech came along with a large camera and a sketch pad. Together we would evaluate the importance of Loretto.

The dark railing was beautiful and still in great shape from its origin in 1878. Indeed, there were no signs of nails, joining, or blending of wood. We took photos from every angle, and John even cut off a tiny piece of wood to do a carbon dating sample. At best, we could see the railing was old, well kept, and not tampered with by the faithful and the unfaithful. We were there for over twelve hours and could find no real reason from the wood samples why this hanging railing could exist, let along stand up the unassisted way it did.

We were simply going to report back to the Archbishop that the swirling stairs had no physical reason for standing as they did. It was the Church's way of saying it was somewhat worthy of veneration. As I left, an old man came forward to close the chapel. He had taken care of it for years we were told, and he smiled at me as I exited. *What did he know, I didn't?* I called him directly over and asked him if he understood how the staircase got up to the top of the apex. He nodded, "José."

"What?"

"José did it in a week of time by himself."

"When can I meet this man?"

"Ah, the Indians say that he came here one night and then later he left, not even paid by the sisters."

"But there are no seams in it."

"Yes, and no nails either."

"Where can I see José?"

"Who knows, he came and went."

"José, Joseph, a carpenter? Is this a joke?"

"What better story did you find here?"

And so that night I went back to the hotel room, and the door was promisingly open. I walked in, and the newspaper reporter was in a slight night gown. As she smiled, I moved closer to her. She asked politely how my meeting had gone.

I told her the whole story over and over again that night. And the next week the AP had a front-page story of the railing's history and a picture of the swirling unsupported wood stairs.

24. THE ORDINARY DUTIES OF THE DAY

(To Frrich)

In December 2000, Al Gore and George Bush were fighting for the presidency, and I was fighting for my life. For seven weeks of hospitalization, my wife would faithfully visit me daily, and the college chaplain who was also the nearby pastor would frequently arrive as well. In the seven weeks he gave me the Catholic Last Rites three times, and when I was unconscious he gave me unconditional absolution for my sins. I later asked him what that meant, and he said it forgave all my transgressions without penance up to that very date. I said I was 56 at the time. "What happens after that?" His response was simple, "After that you're on your own!"

Over the years he became not just a chaplain and a pastor, but a dear friend. As I recuperated, he gave me a copy of a long paperback diary by a Polish nun who had become the first new Catholic saint of the twenty-first century. The chaplain was Polish American, and the nun was a native of Poland. Sister Faustina Kowalska died at 32 of tuberculosis just before the war started in Central Europe in 1939. She was later canonized by a Polish pope. I once kiddingly said I was watching a Polish conspiracy. I am not much for reading devotional literature, but I made it through the 600-page diary. Her major message was simple—the unconditional mercy of Jesus. In his church the chaplain had a banner which read from St. John's Gospel, "I have not come to judge man but to forgive him." What happened to the harsh God of my youth? From her visions, she provided special prayers, and new feasts and even a portrait of Jesus as she saw him. The Polish troops in World War II and in the death camps carried the image with them through the war, and later when some of them immigrated to America. The chaplain created the first Divine Mercy shrine in the commonwealth of Massachusetts, but I had never heard of her or of the diaries.

After two years, I became fascinated with the diary and created a one-woman verse play based on it. In order to be declared a saint in the Church, one must have at least two verifiable miracles attributed to the candidate's intervention. Usually in our times a miracle involves changes in physical conditions of terminal illnesses. It is odd, I have thought, *How the Church so often thought to be the enemy of science since poor Galileo, is so dependent on medical specialists, usually non-Catholic, to verify its canonization process.* In Faustina's case, the first miracle was the remission of terminal Milroy's disease in a heroic woman who had had 60 operations. Then she and her devout husband went to Faustina's crypt in Kracow, and the next day her symptoms went away. American specialists confirmed what happened.

The chaplain generously invited me to meet her and her husband for lunch in middle Massachusetts where a shrine to Faustina has been recently been built. Our guest apparently had prayed for me during my seven terrible weeks in the hospitals and the long convalescence after. She and her husband were decent and lively people committed to the cause of Divine Mercy and to the Year of Mercy proclaimed by Pope Francis. I know my non-Catholic friends are totally turned off by talk of miracles, relics, indulgences, saints, statues, and the traditional ways of the folk Catholicism. *But there she sat to my right, talking to me, swapping Church gossip, and handing me those little butter balls, lightly salted. I saw what I saw.* It was a fascinating lunch and I was truly impressed and grateful for the invitation. When it was over she movingly kissed me on the cheek.

But the night before, I talked quietly with the chaplain whose personal record was partially known to me. He once put up on the entrance to his church a sign, "All are welcome." I sarcastically said to him that he needed a postscript, "Except those divorced, who have had abortions, who practice birth control." He laughed, but little did I know that he was waging his own war for other people's salvation. Neighboring pastors sent women who had abortions to him for confession, fearing that they would get a reputation as being too easy on serious sinners. He supported initial church statements on a gay ministry, and asked me to write the Papal Nuncio in Washington, D.C., a letter as a college president supporting the tolerant proclamation the bishops penned, called "All Our Children," which the Vatican of John Paul II ordered crushed. The chaplain permitted the owner of a strip bar to sing in the church choir, explaining to me simply, "He had a good voice." It reminded me of Jesus calling forth a tax collector to his inner circle.

He told a couple of my students living together to forego sex during Lent, which they did at least probably until Easter Sunday. He confidentially let an old divorced woman who desperately wanted to receive communion before she passed away to confess her sins and then go to Communion. Her husband went with her, and the chaplain buried him in the rites of the church at the end. For all these acts of charity he paid a price, as he became a target of conservative Catholic websites. When he appeared before a state legislative committee in Boston opposing a bill to curtail gay rights, he and a lonely Jesuit theologian stood exposed. The conservative blog sites asked for his dismissal from the priesthood, and zealots appealed to the bishop. He left his parish and his college ministry to go into a ministry dedicated to orders of aged nuns, and worn down vets with post-traumatic stress syndrome, alcoholism and drugs, and circulated among the lost and the bewildered. To a crude biker, he told him the secret of salvation, Faustina's slogan: "Jesus I trust in you," and the guy got to saying it every day. He devoted his life to the problems of poverty just in time to catch the teachings of Pope Francis. Suddenly his near heresies became the new orthodoxy of the vicar of Peter.

I listened intently for quite a while that night to him, and realized another irony in my strange life. I had come all the way to Massachusetts on a hot August day to meet one of the most important people in St. Faustina's life. It was, of course, a rare honor. But listening to him, I saw a real saintly man who was dedicated to the type of deeds she advocated in a life of mercy. I realized that saints on earth do not necessarily have to do the extraordinary curings, special visions, the miracles of the old times, but they are the people around me who "do well the very ordinary duties of the day."

25. A VETERAN OF A FOREIGN WAR

I began my teaching career in September 1970 in Buffalo at the tender age of 25, with a newly minted Ph.D., and a new bride. It was good to be alive and engaged for the first time in experimenting with different modes of pedagogy. Some of the students were in fact my age, and one department secretary refused to let me use the department photocopy machine, not believing I was a faculty member!

I decided for the second semester to move away from the lectures and into an Oxbridge preceptorial system, where I would meet the students one on one, and assign papers for them to research. One of my students ended up working in the White House under Vice President Gore, one is still heading a Republican group of fundraisers, but it was one veteran who I remember the most.

He was 23, and had been drafted and spent two years in Vietnam. And now he was taking advantage of the GI Bill of Rights and went to the local state college hoping to change his life. For some reason he took my course on presidential decision-making. In it, each student would have to do three mini-sized papers on a presidential decision. I had had vets before, but he seemed different in many ways.

I asked him at the first meeting, "Why are you taking an upper division course since you are only a freshman?"

He said, "I desperately want to understand the decisions made by Kennedy, Johnson, and Nixon that got us into Nam." Most of my student vets talked about the battles they were in. Actually their firefights were few and far between.

They recalled the movements of their platoons on the Ho Chi Minh trail, how Nixon saved lives by carpet bombing Cambodia, how they aimlessly sprayed Agent Orange over the poppy fields. But my vet, Alex, spoke of the people in the villages, of the small size of the children with their large eyes and thin bodies, of the young women who looked like little girls, and how he yearned for leave days. He wanted to know why the presidents would order the killing of those kids and of his colleagues. He wanted to understand these presidents' minds and see why they had approved the slaughter.

He began with Kennedy, architect of the fiasco. One day he came in to give me his first paper, and he arrived with a pretty brunette, hippy-type girl, and he told me, "This is my new lady."

The next time I saw him, she was a vapor. I asked him, "What happened to her?"

He said, "I told her that while in Da Nong I had contracted gonorrhea, and she left." He couldn't get an appointment in the VA hospital in Buffalo for six months. I reached into my desk, and gave him a card for a local doctor. I told him he was a friend and would take care of everything, including the costs. Actually, I paid for the visit. There are many ways to get gonorrhea.

As he absorbed himself in Vietnam, he wanted to examine Johnson and the height of the war more closely, and was shocked when he learned that the first week he was president, LBJ told Senator Richard Russell that the war could not be won. Period. Why, Alex, wanted to know did it go on and on?

I did not know, but let him clear his way through the hostile academic underbrush, the way he had gone through the real underbrush in Nam. We talked though of the presidents, and of the war, the sanctity of life, the tension of war guilt, the differences between the Holocaust and the burning of villages, so called pacification. He let me know he had an M-16 at home, a war trophy he sarcastically called it.

He seemed though to become more upbeat, like he was coming out of a tunnel. The last time I saw him he was enjoying himself, and thanked me for the doctor's name. "I feel clean again, I really do. I wonder if she will take me back? I don't think so, once you're scarred, it stays with you. My mother calls it 'the mark of Cain.'"

A week later, the department chairman came to see me, "You know that last night Alex Potter killed himself?"

"What?"

"Yeah, he killed himself in his one bedroom flat over on Elmwood Avenue. He shot his heart out with an M-16, right under a statute of a Buddha. Probably brought it back with him from the East."

I sat frozen. I just seen him and he looked contented. *What if I had been more alert to his words, listened closer to what he wasn't saying, empathized more with retired vets, tried to help him make sense with a word or even a gesture.*

Then the chair remarked, "You know, Mike, sometimes in life we go on with only one leg."

I never taught the Oxbridge preceptor format again. It is too hurtful to get that close to students.

26. THE JERSEY CITY TOUR

Even the most primitive society, anthropologists conclude, celebrates or memorializes the death of a person. How far back that goes in our historical consciousness is unclear, but the remembrance is part of our collective psyche.

The nuns who taught us used to say proudly, "There was a Catholic church on every corner of Jersey City." For older women, the local church was the center of much of their lives, and groups gravitated around its events, its liturgies, its associations. Like many women, their world leisurely revolved especially around wakes and weddings. Each morning the ladies went to the local grocery stores to buy the *Newark Star Ledger* for five cents a copy to read the obituaries and the marriage announcements.

They would go to the churches to see the pomp and circumstance of the weddings and to evaluate the couple sworn to happy matrimony. They would usually go alone or with their daughters, proving that hope springs eternal. The grooms looked like the little men on the top of the bakery wedding cakes. And the brides wore white—a polite fiction for about half of the girls in the neighborhood. The old ladies were rarely invited to the reception, for they did not know the couple, but they just went to see the ceremony.

But wakes were different, depending on the ethnic groups in the rundown Jersey City neighborhoods. The newspapers gave the hours for viewing, for the funerals lasted a laborious three days, supposedly symbolizing the three days of Christ's burial before his Resurrection. On the third day, the final prayers were said, and were followed by an internment and a repast.

The Italians are at heart pagans, and there is a cold finality to the whole affair. The high point of the second evening was when the Capuchin friar began saying the rosary for the sake of the departed. "And so let us begin..." The Italians are a people of deep grief and also people of flowers, so the funeral parlor was covered with huge floral arrangements. The odors were so strong that one could easily be overwhelmed by the sweet smell of flowers mixing promiscuously, so much that forever for me it is the smell of mortality. At the Mass for my Aunt Lucille, the priest gently reminded us that she "who believes in Christ Jesus will live forever." But next to me, my Grandpa, remembering his anti-clerical youth, whispered in Italian, "if He exists?"

Unlike the Italians, the Irish truly believed in God, and turned the wake into a sort of macabre party, full of remembrances, salutations, and toasting.

PLENARY INDULGENCES

My girlfriend in 1969 lost her grandmother Catherine or "Tootsie." She and her group of friends would go from one wake to another, even if they did not know the departed or the family. They dropped by, and after an hour struck up conversations and soon knew they had some people in common, usually friends who had some slow progressing diseases or present medical problems.

But the Irish believed in an afterlife, and their wakes had only a few small floral arrangements, which were somewhat sparse by our standards. When I went to my first Irish wake with my then girlfriend, I was startled when I saw the two brothers and a son gathered around the mahogany coffin, telling jokes and remembering the deceased's crazier, happier moments. I nodded, took a prayer card, and sat in the farthest row away from the coffin. These were not my people. It was a strange night, and the room filled up with the elderly who knew her. The crowd was replete with placemen in the Hague Democratic machine, and most had low level paying jobs in the "organization" as it was called. Cops, firemen, numbers runners, liquor store owners, railroad men, civil servants of every stripe came to pay their respects. At one point one of the local politicians came over to me and put his arm around me, and said, "Ah, Michael, it has been a while since we have seen you in the city." I had never been in the city and never met him. How did he even know my name? "*God, these Irish ward leaders are good*," I thought later.

Up stood the departed's brother, "Big Jack," who took out a collection of plastic cups, a large bottle of whiskey, poured out its contents, and passed them around. He stood up to his full 6'5'' and pronounced a toast, "Ah, to Tootsie, she would have loved to be here." Indeed, she would have.

She had lain aside years ago the dress and shoes she wished to be buried in. Usually it was pink and white, but she changed styles periodically. She was a hypochondriac and in constant communication with the family doctor, except on the day of her life when he forgot to return her call. I had met her only once when her granddaughter and I went up to visit her at the Jersey City Medical Center. She had had a severe stroke and was crippled in bed wearing a loose gown and with full white frizzy hair. Her left side was paralyzed, and she said eerily only one word when I was there, "Light, light, light…." I was uncertain if she was referring to the ugly overhead neon lights or some spiritual epiphany about the apparition of seeking the "way, the truth, the light " that the Gospels call Christ. It probably meant neither. She was facing the darkness, and the light was a sign of fighting the end.

Whenever her husband came in, a railroad man for forty years, she got agitated and started shouting angry syllables. She obviously had a hard feeling toward him for some reason. He was a railroad flagman out of the Jersey City station, then the center of the eastern railroad companies for the whole region. He was Scottish, reticent, morose, kept to himself, and was a bitter contrast to his lively, effervescent wife which earned her the nickname, "Tootsie." She never saw a party she did not enjoy being a part of. He had acquired an early taste for whiskey, and it began to consume his life more and more, and perhaps threatened his marriage bonds as well.

When she died, he sold the house in Jersey City for $8,000, complaining that the neighborhood was "turning," a Jersey euphemism for blacks moving nearby. He retired, got his gold watch from the Pennsylvania Railroad, collected his dependable monthly pension, and moved closer to his son. But his best friend in the new neighborhood was the bartender, and he drank steadily from early morning to late night. Many a time, the son had to pick him up, and charitably bring him home.

Finally the old man decided that he needed a change of scenery, and it was not another town in the doldrums of New Jersey. He had heard from a drinking buddy that there was a cheap, grand cruise for nine days that explored the warm Caribbean. So he made reservations for a private compartment and left for his first real trip. But as he sailed along, he refused to visit the Caribbean islands. He had heard that they were full of black people all over the streets, women with wild headdresses, little half naked children, and unemployed men. So he stayed on the ship, drank, and remembered who did what to him over the years.

A generation later, after he passed away, Jersey City and Hoboken were turning again; they now became the yuppie "gold coast," full of restored dwellings for rich young people who took the easy commute to lower Manhattan where they made money their grandfathers never dreamed of. None of the old timers went back to Jersey City for wakes or funerals anymore.

27. A SENTIMENTAL EDUCATION

First, to get the David Copperfield stuff out of the way. Tom was an entering high school student, 6'1", thin, blond and fairly handsome. He played a good game of basketball, but nothing superlative. In his sophomore year in high school he had a discernment in the Catholic Church's terms, and he decided he would be a priest. He had several girlfriends over the years and even went all the way with one, but his passions became more spiritual and his mild manner led him to the priesthood. His parents counseled him to wait, but he insisted on entering the junior seminary, and then got ready to go to the local diocesan seminary. But to Tom's surprise, the bishop intervened and sent him to the North American College in Rome, the traditional training ground for fast track appointments to the hierarchy.

He was also instructed to take additional courses in canon law at the Angelicum, the famed Dominican retreat house of study on the Quirinal hill where the alumni had included Karl Wojtyla, Pope John Paul II. At first Tom was overwhelmed by the changes and by the vast city of Rome. He was a part of the center of a great international organization, and he felt good just being somehow included. He lived at the North American College on the Janiculum Hill in a spartan room with a small bed, a sink, a tiny desk and a crucifix by the window. In the morning he went to the common bathroom to shower and shave. As he stood over the basin, he could see out the windows the very top of St. Peter's Basilica, a most inspiring way to begin the day. When he entered to take his extra course work at the Angelicum, he was surprised that such an important center inside had such common furnishings. No Renaissance art was in much of the halls and rooms. But the professors were truly experts in their areas, especially canon law. Dominicans were comfortable with the architectonic philosophy of St. Thomas Aquinas, their conferee back in the 13th century. And so he learned their way of thinking, starting off with a set of faith principles and then in lockstep logic coming to conclusions. But where Aquinas was subtle, his twentieth century followers were rigid. Since they had the truth of faith, they moved along to answers. Where Aquinas was influenced by Arabic, Jewish and Greek sources, his latter day students simply followed his journey. They just accepted his conclusions, never knew his sources. One evening one of their finest theologians invited a lay historian who decided to present a case for the extenuating circumstances for birth control, abortion, and gay relationships. The students stood mute as he spoke, and later wanted to know from their teacher if he were serious. He was too far outside of the Thomist paradigm for them, and the professor probably regretted his invitation.

At times Tom missed Minnesota, but he formed friendships easily, and after the awful North American College's dinners, he marched down the hill with the others to a little trattoria in the neighborhood. They easily consumed cheap wine and soon harder stuff, and Tom joined in. In a year he became heavily dependent on liquor to get through the lonely nights. One day, he read Edwin O'Connor's novel *Edge of Sadness*, and realized that he used liquor to get through the afternoons as well. In Rome at out of the way places other seminarians dressed in casual garb were willing to welcome the handsome Tom into their circle.

He was slow to realize the seminarians were part of a small group in the Vatican who maintained close, very personal friendships with each other. One day, Tom stopped in front of the church of the Lateran, the pope's real church as bishop of Rome. There were old ladies and young children going up the steps one by one on their knees. These were supposedly the stairs St. Monica, the mother of Emperor Constantine, brought back from Jerusalem and some say they were the very steps Jesus climbed to this death.

"If these old ladies could do it, so can I," he mumbled and he began his climb. He never realized that knees have so little flesh on them. But he made his way up, stopping and looking through glass circles. The red marks were supposed to be the blood dripped from the Savior himself, type A blood actually.

Once this ancient building was the home of a famous Roman family of the Laterani, and approaching it, he dropped to his knees and began to feel the pain of knowing that he was an alcoholic and was in a scandalous group of men. He went into the church, toward a dark confessional with a sign that said "English," and began his confession.

"Bless me father, for I have sinned. It has been a month since my last confession and I have committed offenses, venial and mortal, against my vows." The priest spoke broken English but understood everything, and was startled when he found out Tom was an American seminarian.

"Americans, huh, you all worry too much about sinning and not enough about God's love and mercy. I alone don't forgive you, but together we are asking God's boundless forgiveness. For your penance, you will visit each of the seven great churches in Rome, and in each say the Lord's Prayer. Do you comprehend? Go, go in peace and in forgiveness."

And so he was out into the dark church and then into the Roman air. He looked at the thick clouds over the city, and somehow he saw overhead the Holy Ghost flying away. *Was it an illusion,* he wondered?

His life was changed though, his vocation more assured; he studied more. He wanted to return home and be a great preacher, and he read the sermons of the English cleric, John Henry Cardinal Newman, but the cardinal's homilies were so eloquent and highbrow. They may have been more useful for the students of Oxford, rather than the working class parishes of Minnesota. He counted on being a great confessor, sort of like St. John Vianney of France, but he could not hear confessions 24 hours a day like he did, and accomplish anything else.

And it continued as he graduated and returned to the Diocese of St. Paul and Minneapolis. He hoped he would be assigned to a parish near his family, but the bishop had other plans. He had not spent all that money in Rome to train a parish curate to teach CYO baseball in St. Paul. He immediately assigned Tom to be the head of the diocesan panel to hear annulment cases. He acquired a reputation for the strict dispensing of his cases, and he was to be the chief adjudicator with little appeal beyond his level. He was replacing an old monsignor who simply checked the box "rejected," believing that preserved the diocese's integrity. It was an appropriate way to apply the Church's prohibition against divorce as best he could. Still Tom was troubled, for the Church used the admonitions of Jesus to reject divorce, but the parable is one of the few in which Jesus' opponents get the best of Him. Since he opposes divorce, the Pharisees reminded him that the old Jewish patriarchs permitted divorce in the Torah. Jesus responded that in those times "men's hearts were hardened." *"Yet can anyone deny those men's hearts are harder than ours today?"* Tom understood.

But he went along, did not expand the conditions for annulments, and shuddered when the nephew of President Kennedy with five kids was granted an annulment by the Archdiocese of Boston, and the nephew called the process a "joke." For what reasons, did he prevail?

Soon after he asked for a transfer to a local parish and in gratitude forgot most of what had happened. Besides the bishop thought the boy who had everything handed to him needed to learn the greatest lesson—humility. So Thomas began life as a lowly curate. The pastor was a genial Irish-American who had bad diabetes so he could barely walk. Physical activities of all types passed to an eager Thomas. He felt comfortable with his people; for he came out of these types of working class neighborhoods, full of the old folk religion that cared little about theology or dogmatic fine points.

Tom was most scrupulous though in hearing confessions. He took the pastor's place as well, and listened to the litany of swearing, lying, and adultery that are the measures of modern men and women on earth. Then one day a young woman came in, and in the darkness of the confessional asked for absolution for one sin—abortion. He was startled; he was sure that only the bishop under canon law could absolve that sin, unless he delegated the power to parish priests. He consoled her, but told her he had to get the bishop's approval. She became quiet, and he asked her to please give him a week. "Please come back, please."

Then he learned that the bishop had indeed delegated that power; how could he have not known, working in the chancellery office? He was so involved in annulments that he never followed the rest of the diocese goings-on.

So he waited a week, all day in the confessional. No one came. He waited a second and a third week. He had lost her soul. A month later he had heard of a suicide of a young woman in the parish, and he feared that it was the same woman, but he never knew. Sadly, guilt came over him, and he was sure he was feeling more and more depressed, more lethargic, and morose, desperately trying to avoid a complete breakdown. When the Christmas season came he was glad, for the happenings would hopefully lift his depression.

He slowly began to see that he was not a judge to administer justice to unworthy people. In his diocese, only 25% of the people even went to church on Sunday; fewer still went to confession. Fellow priests called it the "lost sacrament of penance." One pastor fought back by announcing that he was going to give, in one fell swoop, absolution to all the parishioners at the Mass before Palm Sunday. The church was full that night, but when the bishop heard of his scheme he accused him of violating canon law. Penance was for one person at a time; general confession was reserved for extraordinary cases like soldiers going into combat. But all of us now go into combat every day, and the Church was unsympathetic. But it had been no more supportive of poor Joan of Arc going into battle. She was burnt at the stake and is now a saint.

But Tom's "Dark Night of the Soul" had changed him from a young canon lawyer to a pastoral figure. In confession, an old Italian lady, who had married at 20, now had three fine kids, but confessed that they was from her second marriage. Her first husband in the first month of their marriage had hit her regularly, his idea of foreplay. As Freud, said sadism and eroticism are often bound up.

In total fright, the young bride left him and went home to her family. She tried to get an annulment in the diocese; but this was her true marriage and she had to get a civil divorce. She wanted all her life to take communion at their daughter's wedding. The church's view on absolution was solid she was told. Tom knew even the statute number of canon law, but for some reason he told her to say an act of contrition to the Blessed Virgin, who especially understood the sufferings of women. And so the old mother left the confessional in the good graces of the Church.

As he began to generally absolve women who had had abortions, usually young and poor woman, he noticed that timid priests in the area sent their parishioners to his confessional to hear and judge their lives. And he began to talk of God's mercy and love, and how He gave the greatest mercy to the greatest sinners. They told him long stories of how they wanted to come back to the church, bringing their children, and had nightmares of what the abortive baby could look like. Some wondered if he would be another Beethoven or one who cured cancer. Tom led them through the tunnel to the other side, and in the process he sawed off canon law.

When the bishop decided to launch a political offensive against homosexuality and also same sex marriage, Tom was uncomfortable calling a child or an adult "inherently degraded" morally. He proposed a gay conference, had gay retreats, educated himself on gay life, and even in his darkest hours reminded himself of the Vatican cell of homosexuals in Rome.

He became less judgmental and more merciful. But his views were not popular in the diocese and his brilliant career was over as bishops changed. Sending him to the North American College, one said, was a waste of money. But he knew his Aquinas too well, and they would not debate him. After all in clerical circles, gossip is the common currency of discussion.

Then in 2012 as he was coming to the end of his active vocation, the new pope, from the New World, was thinking of allowing divorced Catholics to take communion. After much consultation, he issued a statement that was so ambiguous and confusing that all sides thought it enshrined their view; the pope was a Jesuit, who enjoyed the activist soldier Ignatius rather than the scholar Aquinas.

Suddenly, Tom's wayward advice was becoming the new orthodoxy. When the pope was asked about the gays in the Vatican, he shrugged it off, "Who am I to judge?" The Vatican said his remarks were taken out of context. Of course, the pope judges—he is paid to judge. That is why we have canon law that so preoccupied Tom when he was young. When the pope was told that a cadre of conservative cardinals wanted his apology for confusing the laity, he said, "I don't lose sleep over them."

And so neither did Thomas. He slept soundly, sleeping the sleep not of the just, but of the merciful.

28. VISITOR

(in verse)

I did not know her well, but she knew me.
She was an alumna of our college
Who worked for Al Gore.
A nice job for a young graduate,
A fine stepping stone beyond.
She was pleasant, plain looking,
A local girl who was a simple
Staff person to the number two guy.
She read my history of the presidency,
And invited me to a personal tour
Of the White House at night,
When it was dark outside,
All the blazing lights were on,
And so I went past endless security
To meet her, and then we went up to the
Oval Office. The president was away,
We could walk in, it really is oval,
And it is surprisingly small, with six doors
That are cut into the molding of the walls.
Where they lead who knows.
But all I could think was Lincoln walked
Back and forth and pondered the terrible war.
Here FDR wheeled his chair and smoked his cigarettes
Up tilted, and entertained the most hostile people,
As if he cared about them.
The outside doors lead to the portico,
The air was cold and wet,
We walked around as if we belonged there,
And I saw one of Clinton's open books,
He was reading my second volume
He wanted to be a great president,
But he never would
For he was too familiar with where the doors

Opened up to, and too preoccupied with
The trappings of privilege
And not the greatness of the men
Whose portraits he had hung on the wall.
They worried about the people,
Trying to complete the unfinished agenda
Of their generations. It got colder and darker,
As if I could see Bull Run and the Battle of the Bulge
With them in the nation's night.

MICHAEL P. RICCARDS

29. VERDI COMES TO TOWN

The greatest Italian composer of the century, Giuseppe Verdi, was traveling back from a vacation along the Adriatic Sea to the Naples opera house. He was riding in a regal coach with two horses, taking him through many back picturesque roads which would pass near the small town of Rotunda. The people there had heard about his trip, and were delighted that he would be nearby. They wanted to welcome him and, although they did not have an opera house in that little town, they did have a full uniformed band.

Verdi was not just a composer, he was appointed a senator in the new unified Italy. During the period of Bourbon cruelties, his work had at the time been censored, but he was wily in avoiding the authorities. To symbolize his allegiance to the Italian Risorgimento, the revolution, he penned an opera called *Nabucco* which involved the famed chorus "l'pensiero," lamenting the captivity of the Hebrew slaves by the pharaoh. That tune became the unofficial anthem of the Risorgimento throughout the peninsula. Even his name became an anagram in Italian, **V**ittorio **E**manuele **re** d'**I**talia *(*Long live Victorio Emmanuel, King of Italy). When the revolution was successful, as much as anything can be successful in Italy, Verdi became a national hero.

But national heroes have responsibilities, so he accepted the kind invitation to visit Rotunda and lead a parade through the center of town, stopping for a brief but sumptuous lunch. One of the onlookers was my grandfather, then only ten years old, but an aficionado of bands and music. Raffaele's family had no money left at the end of the month so he never learned to play an instrument or even sing. Still he was going to the Giuseppe Verdi parade and was fated to walk at its end. His forebears had been allies of the patriots, and for a while hid the currency plates of the Risorgimento. The Spanish Bourbon governor learned of the treachery and tortured the members of the family by burning the soles of their feet. They still refused to tell the conquerors the fate of the plates, and the family became local heroes.

The very aged Maestro Verdi, armed with his top hat and weary at the end of a long journey, met the town celebrities, graciously bowed at their presence, and took from the bandleader the glorious baton, and he started to lead the band down a dusty main street to the town square. He, of course, started with the chorus from *Nabucco*, which everybody knew and all sang as they marched.

84

Va, pensiero, sull' ali dorate;
Va, ti posa sui clivi, sui colli,
Ove olezzano tepide e molli,
L'aure dolci del suolo natal!
Del Giordano le rive salute,
Di Sionne le torri atterrated.
Oh, mia patria si bella e perduta!
Oh, membranza si cara e fatal![1]

As they went past the local Catholic church, the parish priest was ordered by the bishop to turn his back on the Italian flag. It symbolized the new Italy, the new Italian state, which had conquered the Papal States. But he was alone and Verdi was an anti-cleric anyhow.

In the plaza the people laid out tables of delicacies which the women had

---

[1]Fly, thought, on wings of gold,
Go settle upon the slopes and the hills
Where the sweet airs of our
Native soil smell soft and mild!
Great the banks of the river Jordan
And Zion's tumbled towers.
Oh my country, so lovely and lost!

proudly made. "Viva Verdi," they cried, and he responded, "Viva l'Italia." At the luncheon the mayor casually told the story to the maestro of the bravery of the Finelli family. He pointed to his descendant, little Raffaele, who stood quietly over in the corner. As the party ended, Verdi rose with the baton and then stopped. He called the boy over and asked him to walk with him in the front, carrying the red, white and green flag of the republic. Raffaele was proudly now in front.

They returned by the same parade route, and Verdi struck up the Hebrew slaves' song once again, but he pointed to Raffaele and told him to carry high the Italian flag as they retraced the march. As they moved forward the maestro turned to Raffaele and said, "You have a good voice, and the mayor tells me you come from patriotic stock. What more could an Italian boy want?" Raffaele proudly marched by Verdi down the dirt road to his horses and elegant carriage. Once there the band continued to play tunes from *Il Trovatore* and *La Traviata* as Verdi took off his top hat and waved grandly. It was act five once again.

He heard them shouting, "Viva Verdi. Viva l'Italia," and was helped into the carriage and drove off. The band leader raised the baton Verdi had ceremoniously given back to him. They all marched home, Raffaele still carrying the Italian flag high, the red symbol of bravery, the white purity of motive, the green the beauty and hope of nature.

THE PLAYS

THE CONFESSIONS OF ST. PATRICK

To Dr. Lawrence McCullough and the Irish People Everywhere

THE CONFESSIONS OF ST. PATRICK

IRISH BARD: (*center stage singing*)

Red Rose, proud Rose, sad Rose of all my days!
Come near me, while I sing the ancient ways:
Cuchulain battling with the bitter tide;
The Druid, grey, word-nurtured, quiet-eyed,
Who cast round Fergus dreams, and ruin untold;
And thine own sadness, where of stars, grown old
In dancing silver-sandalled on the sea,
Sing in their high and lonely melody.
Come near, that no more blinded by man's fate,
I find under the boughs of love and hate,
In all poor foolish things that live a day,
Eternal beauty wandering on her way.

Come near, come near, come near—Ah, leave me still
A little space for the rose-breath to fill!
Lest I no more hear common things that crave;
The weak worm hiding down in its small cave,
The field mouse running by me in the grass,
And heavy mortal hopes that toil and pass;
But seek alone to hear the strange things said
By God to the bright hearts of those long dead,
And learn to chant a tongue men do not know.
Come near; I would, before my time to go,
Sing of old Eire and the ancient ways:
Red Rose, proud Rose, sad Rose of all my days.

PATRICK:
I, Patrick, a sinner—
The most rustic and unworthy
Among all God's faithful,
Was born to Calpornius, a deacon
Of the Roman Church, the son of Potitus, a priest.
The family had a sprawling estate
Near Bannaventa Berniae.

91

The house was built of rough stone,
For stone is easier to come by
Than wood and long-stemmed nails.
The land belonged in Celtic Britain,
The far edges of the Roman Empire,
And of the devout Roman Church.
In the cold damp winters, we burnt
The greenish brown clumps of moss.
It barely kept us warm.
I hate the chill, the cold, the aching
Feeling of wet winters.
For that is the inner circle of hell,
It is not fire or flames,
But the cold that seeps
Into your tired bones,
And never goes away
Until the spring sun does come.
My father wore a bleached white tunic
With a simple purple stripe,
And became a married deacon,
To enjoy the pleasures of the flesh,
And the tax exemptions of the clergy.
We were noble born,
And noble bred in the time of Theodosius,
The Spaniard who destroyed the heresies
And ended forever the pagan Olympic Games.

Our outpost town had a forum,
Where rowdy meetings and bawdy plays
Were presented near the bathhouse.
There were still temples to Mithras,
The seat of the blood-soaked bull,
And to Celtic gods: Teutates,
Maponus, and Brigantia.

We spoke in Latin and in early British.
As a boy I heard of ancient warriors,
Haughty proud and strikingly handsome,
Of giants and ugly monster men,
And of a magical cup of history,
The holy grail of Joseph of Arimethea,
The chalice of the Last Supper.
Riverrun through Eve and Adam,
We are British from the beginning.
My mother was a dedicated Christian.
But I was since childhood

A firm and devout…atheist.
I believed in the future, my future,
But not the Christian God,
Or the gods of the blood-drenched bull.
No god would visit on us
Such damp and lasting cold.

In my youth, I committed
A grave and unforgettable sin,
All my life its shadow
Followed me, until my end.
Even after I was a bishop
I believed in mercy,
But how dark and deep
It is, branded into my soul.
I have forgiven many of their sins:
Pride, lust, robbery,
Sodomy, blasphemy,
But this is so pressed into my heart.
At fifteen, my life was marked forever.
I enjoyed the life of the idle rich,
Of the noble born son
Of a fine patrician,
A landholder and official,
Of the Roman Empire,
Of the Catholic Church
With its rites and rituals.

Father made us go to the endless Masses,
Not in British but incense-smelling Latin.
The gospels according to Matthew and Mark,
Luke and John, but most importantly Paul.
These others sat in libraries
Feasting on holy days,
But Paul went by mule and ship
All over the Gentile world,
Preaching the gospel before
There was a single Gospel written.

I did not believe in God,
But I fiercely admired
A man who created a bond
Between Jesus and himself,
For he created the Church.

And then it happened one warm night,

As I dozed off to a groggy sleep.

VOICE:
Chain the boy and take only the healthy,
Leave the old and very young,
Enjoy the women for pleasure,
But take the strong
To our sacred isle.

PATRICK:
Across the Irish Sea, we rode
In iron chains, into the east coast.
Boys cried and screamed for mama,
But in several days' time
We rolled beyond the waves
To where the *hiera* dwelled.
On ship we quietly talked:
It was a land of cannibals
Who ate their own,
A frozen island on the edge of the world.
They have sex with their mothers and sisters,
Their cattle explode from over-eating.
It was an island where even
The smallest birds do not live.
Irish bite off the nipples and asses
Of shepherds and their luckless wives.
It was a special treat for the Irish.
Oddly, the master made me a shepherd,
To tend and watch his herds,
To move them to pasture,
To corral them at night,
I slept, and hummed,
And declaimed, and whistled
To the sleepy sheep on the land.
The island is so flat,
So gentle, so green
Where we were enslaved.

I did not have a harp,
I could not compose a psalm,
Like the boy David outside the city
Of ancient Bethlehem
Where he was born and raised.
Though I walk through the valley
Of death, I will fear no evil.
My master gave me a staff,

Like David used in his walks.

I was so alone, alone,
With only chants in my mind,
And in my artless soul.

VOICE:
And then one night
You heard me, not a vision,
Not an apparition,
But a presence you felt
Come like a thief in the night.

PATRICK:
At first, I heard voices
From the woods of Foclot
Now the western sea of the holy island.

VOICE:
Rise up and follow the shore line,
There will be a rusty cargo ship,
The captain will know you
Even if he does not know you.

PATRICK:
That made no real sense,
But I hid away food pieces
And some more cloaks,
Took my shepherd dog
To a neighboring farm,
And let him frolic,
While I departed.

VOICE:
Hurry, hurry,
Come follow me.

PATRICK:
The shore, I sensed, was far far away.
I walked toward the rising sun,
Being led by a blowing wind.
I knew the ship's sails
Need the gusts to get in the sea.
I followed the wind for weeks,
Eating often from the land's few trees,
Some 180 miles, I walked.

I saw other places along the way,
And wished in part I had a mare.
Oh, horseman pass by.
Young ladies and their lovers
Coming together and quietly apart.
I came upon at night
A den of wolves,
And wondered if I had come this far,
To be ripped apart
In the name of an uncaring God?

VOICE:
Come, follow me.

PATRICK:
The wolves are in fact the sons
Of the prince of darkness.
Ireland is full of demons,
It is full of monsters,
And rich pagan gods.
Ireland is a pack of heathens.
The land began to sink,
And there on the morning mist,
Was a collection of ships,
Mostly from Britain, I assumed.
Now, how to get an obvious fugitive
On board as a worker,
For they could call the bailiff,
And I would be a slave again,
And they would be richer for no effort.

I spoke in British,
With an Irish sound,
I had spent too much time on the farm,
And we spoke no Latin.
But what seaman ever
Read Virgil or spoke Cicero?

"Captain, are you short a hand,
For I am a sturdy man,
Looking for the sea's adventure."

"You from around here?"

"No, far away, far away,
But this is the closest

The sea comes to my place."

"You look big and strong, my boy,
Get on board, we leave in an hour."

VOICE:
Behold your ship is ready.

PATRICK:
I did not know which ship at first
To choose for my voyage,
But a voice told me to go,
And go I did on the Celtic Runner.
I was so tired from the walk,
But I worked harder and faster
Than any on board.
My captain took many days
For a short trip—
We stopped to pick up barley,
Corn, potatoes and Irish crafts.
For the British love primitive arts.
I loaded and unloaded.
Is this what the Christian God
Had in mind for me,
After my long march to the sea?
Little wonder He has so few
Real friends on earth.
But I thought back
To the days of my slavery,
How God used this time
To shape and mold me
Into something better than before.
I came to care about others,
And work to come to their assistance.
Before I was a slave,
I didn't even care for myself.
I was like a stone stuck
Deep in a mud puddle,
But God came along
And pulled me out.
I would remember slowly,
Ever slowly the stories of the Bible,
Especially the chants
Of the shepherd boy of Bethlehem,
And the woes of Job
Whom God forgot.

I was up at sunrise,
And said a hundred prayers every morning
Then a hundred at night.
The Irish farm lads
Called me "holy boy."
Then I began to fast,
Hold back on food and drink,
Mortify my body,
So as to praise my God.
And the Irish made humor of it all.
And then:

VOICE:
You have fared well,
You will be home again.

PATRICK:
The sailors on board had
The boys sucking on their breasts,
It was — they said — adoption,
Bonding to the crew,
But I was told it was a pagan rite,
And I did not do it for fear of God.
On the twentieth day we lacked food
And hunger made us weak.
The captain cried out,
"Christian boy, what are you going to do.
If your God is great,
Why not pray for our relief.
We are dying of starvation,
And will never see another soul."

"Your heart must turn toward Him,
Nothing is impossible for God.
Today He will send you food,
Into your right path—
Fill your bellies,
His abundance will be ours soon,"
And so it happened.

It was not like manna in the desert,
For surely I was no Moses.
And there ahead of us
Was a stray large herd
Of prime pigs,
Yes, pigs!

Unlike the chosen people,
The Israelites of Moses,
The Celtic people loved pork,
And these are the trailings
Of an unruly herd.
We landed, killed, and feasted,
But now I was a prophet
Among the heathens.
Even the few dogs with us
Ate well that day.
And the crew found wild honey
And with respect offered me some,
One crew man said—
"We have dedicated this as a
Sacred sacrifice to the gods."
But since I believed in the One,
I would not partake of it.
Quietly in the days to follow
They would come and ask me,
"Tell us of the Christ god-man."
And I did.

But seeing those rough sailors gathering,
And even praying, one night
The evil one attacked me
As I lay asleep.
He jumped on my chest
Like a great huge rock,
And I could not move my legs,
Or my arms, and I was pinned.
"Satan, off me, begone Satan."
But he stayed.
Then I cried out, "Elijah, Elijah!"
Out came the rage of the sea,
Then at night, the pain
Went away, the weight lifted,
And I beheld Christ Jesus,
Who saved my body and soul that night.

Oh, Lord Christ the son,
Watch over me, watch over my eyes,
My throat, my heart, my legs,
But mostly dear Jesus watch over my soul,
Cleave to me,
Like I herded my flock,
Herd me.

For you are the Good Shepherd,
And I know mine,
And mine knows me.
We landed, and disembarked,
And carried the goods to the edge
Of the British port,
And seamen got drunk
And looked for paid women
Who would spend in one night
Their meager wages.
I left quickly, up the docks,
And then into the hinterlands,
I knew my destination—
For it was home.

It was now a balmy autumn day,
I approached Bannaventa Berniae,
Our family villa in the sweet distance.
My pulse grew more rapid,
My heart beat irregularly.
My God, it looked the same,
But I did not, after six slave years.
I approached the front gate,
And there was my boyhood dog,
Limping now with age,
But quick to recognize me.

I felt like Ulysses,
Being seen first by his dog.
Gratefully he whined,
He barked, he licked my face.
I was his master home again.
My father heard the noise,
And thought it was the dog again,
But as he came closer
His dim eyes saw a ghost, his son once dead
Is alive again.
Lay the plates for a feast,
The prodigal son has returned.
He cried out for my mother,
Who came in fright, and then in awe,
She even hugged me,
And then dropped to her knees
Like she had seen the Resurrected Christ.

She was never a nonbeliever,

She kept the faith,
But now beyond her dreams,
Her dead son was back again.
She recognized me,
But then did not,
For I was her boy become a man,
I was changed, and she sensed it,
For like any good mother,
She knew that my soul had been scarred
By six years, by being a slave,
But leaving with only a boy's faith,
The Bible, some prayers, a baptism.
I was yet to be confirmed,
Most of my playmates were married,
With children of their own,
And I at twenty-one was in tatters,
With a dirty beard,
And powerful shoulders and back,
Like only a laboring man can earn.
No son of a patrician
Had those calluses,
No son of this village
Had ever wrestled Satan and won,
No son of these people
Had ever dared say:
For your boys will have visions,
And your old men will dream dreams.
So I never said anything at first.
The word went out quickly—
For the family called together a feast,
Drink flowed,
The British beer was all present,
There were sweets of all sorts,
And young women arrived
To hear a man tell tales of his travels.
Somehow they did not see me
As a slave returned,
But as a ship master
Set sail across the edge of the sea.
What were the Irish savages like?
The priests wanted to know
If they were indeed cannibals.
Did they know of the Gospels,
Did they know of baptism,
Did they have some sort of marriage,
Or did they couple like dogs?

Did they eat what we do,
And drink beer and fine whiskey?
Had they lived up on the edge
Of the great Roman Empire?
Father saw I was weary,
And so he led me gently
To my old room—
There it was as before,
They had not touched it.
The bed, the drawers,
The drapes all were as I remembered them,
I carefully locked the window,
For it was through there I was captured
Six long years ago,
And at my feet
The old dog lay happy and tired,
For it was a good day
Of sweet, sweet remembrance.

VOICE:
Now what is he to do?
He is home and must set a path.

PATRICK:
I was changed in many ways
The family could never understand.
I was a ghost come running over the glen,
At first I walked every English yard,
I would sit on a rock,
Oh, how this land is so rocky,
And I sang out
The blessed psalms of King David,
Done when he was a shepherd boy.
He played the lyre,
He roamed with the flocks
Who bunched together
In a round group
As the dogs snapped at their heels.
Now Father Time nipped at my heels.
I was only twenty-one, but felt a lifetime.
My face was so burned,
My hands so long and wiry,
I was not a British prince,
But a Celtic man,
Still in so many ways a slave.
But God had found me,

Had He not?
He called out to me.

VOICE:
Patrick, come follow me…

PATRICK:
But I am a sinner,
I have committed acts
So grievous that even
Your Divine Mercy cannot abide.

VOICE:
I can forgive all,
I see all, I know all.
No sin is beyond My reach.
You are only a slave
In your mind,
Give up your chains
And follow me,
Stop thinking of suicide,
You'd damn your immortal soul,
And still I am with you,
Even beyond the consummation of the world.
Do my work, save your soul,
Be buried in sacred ground.

PATRICK:
Around us was the empire
Crumbling, all is destruction.
Nothing is immortal.
Nothing matters,
Even my youth was a lie,
The father of my father was a lie.

VOICE:
Even if you swear at me,
Deny me, doubt me
You know I freed you
Like Moses did the Israelites.
But you already had the Word,
He had to find it.
So I gave it to him,
And I gave you the memory of youth.

PATRICK:
I went home that day disturbed,
God does not speak to me in British,
Least of all of cold and damp Ireland,
I can smell mortality,
Like the old lumps of bogs.

That night I had another vision.
In the mist an old man
Called by the Irish Victoricus,
Carrying a load of letters,
Scrolls with seals
Dropped on my youthful bed.
The first began:
"Patrick, the Voice of the Irish,"
And the voice cried out, "Holy boy,
Come here and walk with us!"

I awoke and would read no more,
Return to my kidnappers!
To my slave hut,
To another master's sheep
To eat swill and bad Irish whiskey!
I must forget
All these dreams and visions,
The curse of the Irish,
I should accomplished great deeds,
Follow my father, love my mother,
Meet her friends' lasses
And do what is natural.
Being natural is surely not
To return to the land of my slavery.
Then as the days passed by
My nights were filled
With horrors and Irish monsters again.
I heard a single voice,
A prayer from God,
Did the words come from my diseased mind,
Or inside me.

VOICE:
The One who gave you your spirit,
It is He who speaks to you.

PATRICK:
Father, mother, I am to be a priest.

And they said,
"Fine, your grandfather was one,
We will build you a grand chapel
Here near us, or in the town square.
The Christians are good people,
But we are still a new sect,
We cannot even recite
Our common beliefs yet,
Who are truth tellers,
Who are the heretics?
We do not know,
Except to love Christ Jesus.
Stay here with us,
Train to be a holy priest,
Marry, forgive sins,
Study with Germanus,
The bishop who visits us often.

I did stay home and study,
I knew I would not be
Just a married priest,
But a devoted bishop.
I traveled to Gaul,
To Italy and to the Tyrrhenian isles.
Then I went to the great monasteries,
Listened to their elegant Latin,
And retraced in part the voyage
Of St. Paul, Apostle to the Gentiles.
I was ordained,
And then sought to ordain others,
To become bishop of Ireland,
To spread the faith.

The Irish had a bishop,
Palladius, who came and went.
He hated the people and the isle.
He was a Gaullist at heart,
And left ignominiously.
He said the wild men of Ireland
Would not listen to his preaching,
And he died on the way home.
The new Pope Celestine needed a bishop,
But no ambitious clergymen
Would go to the dark island
Near the edge of the world.

There were already some bishops,
Priests and dedicated missionaries,
And they wrestled like Job
Over whether to recognize me,
But God used His will,
And I became the primate.
I visited the remote parts,
To the very northern shores,
What lay beyond those waters?
Even the empire stopped.
Some tribes like the Picts
Came to Christ, and then left him.
Many converts were slaves,
Looking for comfort,
And women, looking for dignity,
Like the women around the Lord.

The Irish believed in many gods,
Hoping to appease them
And avoid the plagues of the world.
They believed in magic,
Their ancestors, diverse animals,
Reincarnation to other safer lives.

The Christian Church preached outdoors,
In a home, in a barn—
Like the Last Supper, like the Nativity.
We are a simple church in Ireland,
Not like the great churches in Rome,
Built by the empire's taxes,
Built by the great Constantine
And his beloved mother, Helen.

When I first came back to the island,
I was greeted in the weirdest ways
By the Irish pagan priests,
The Druids, the very sons of the Antichrist.
I was still then a rural priest,
But soon I confronted them
At the festival of Tara,
Called simply Baal's fire.
The diviners of Erin predicted
"New days of peace shall come,
Which shall endure forever.
The country of Temor shall be deserted."

VOICE:
The Druids from Logaire rested,
The coming of Patrick concealed that.
Their predictions were verified
Concerning the king whom they foretold.
"He comes, he comes with shaven crown,
Roam far off the storm-tossed sea,
His garment pieced at the neck
With a cork-like staff comes he,
Far in his house, at the east end,
His cups and patens lie,
The people answer to his voice:
Amen, Amen, they cry,
Amen, Amen."

PATRICK:
Our great Roman conqueror,
Julius Caesar, wrote that in Gaul
The Druids believed in human sacrifice,
Full retribution, and
That they drew up immense figures,
Woven out of twigs,
Filled with their enemies,
And set them aflame.

And so in the Day of Tara,
I went to that city,
So different from where I was,
Each chieftain followed by a tribe,
Would assemble with the priests,
And the Irish bards,
For they loved a good song,
Especially of their own making.

Therein the midst of them,
I, Patrick, a sinner,
The bishop of all Ireland,
Would raise up a cross
Of the crucified and risen Christ.
If I failed to sway the masses
I would be a bloody victim of Druids.
We ascended the hill of Slane,
All fires were prohibited,
But then I set aflame
The twigs and drew down Druid wrath.
I was seized by their followers,

As they carried me and their black flag.
There I appeared on the plain,
Before the high king,
Dressed in a plain white tunic,
I was calm and possessed by God Himself,
And King Logaire who commanded silence,
I spoke knowing that he like all men
Was weighed by guilt and feared punishment.
I talked of sin and its terrors,
And he listened.
"Do not fear the terrors of the night,
Do not let the Druid altars bear your sacrifice.
Do they give you comfort,
Or peace of mind?
Has guilt left you,
What say your heart?
Flee from their altars
And come find Christ.
These blood sacrifices pollute the bearer,
See I have a better altar,
A greater sacrifice etched by the Father.
I tell you all of the good news,
A message of good and love,
Of compassion and sweet mercy."

And so they began turning away
From the Baal, on the Day of Tara.
The minister of state said nothing.
The king talked little,
But his wife and daughter came over to the cross.
Day next, the king's brother came to me.
Then the chief of the bards, Dubbach.
Logaine still said little,
But he never traveled with the Druids again.
That is the tale of Tara.

And I recalled Cuchulain,
The great Irish pagan hero,
And he helped me to convert the high end.
I had summoned Cuchulain from hell,
For he had done much evil in his brave life.
I rewarded him with a free pass to Heaven,
And so he supported me before the king.

The devil Corra fought me
For forty days and nights as I fasted,

I then threw my silver bell at her,
And she burnt it and fled.
Holding the black bell high,
I banned all the snakes
From Ireland forever,
And created the Celtic Cross.
By laying a pagan sun over a cross,
So the Irish realized it was theirs.

The devil had dropped a boulder
At Cashel and I founded a church there.
When the unbelievers mocked the Trinity,
I showed them the shamrock—
Three become one.

As I sat with my clergy
By the well in the Rath of Crogas.
Two beautiful sassy daughters
Of the King of Connaught approached.

VOICE:
Why are you here, Patrick?

PATRICK:
I answered "You had better come
To confess in God rather than talk of me."

VOICE:
Who is God?

PATRICK:
I tell you He is the Creator of life,
The Redeemer of Sins. He knows
Your hearts better than your father does!
And so I baptized them.

A blessing in every mouth.
A blessing in every mount and vale,
Glen and ridge,
I bent myself to a new strength,
A calling of the Holy Trinity.

I preached:
God's power to uphold me,
God's wisdom to guide me,
God's eye to see before me.

God's ear can hear me,
God's work to speak for me,
God's hand to guide me.

All condemned the false prophets,
The heathens, the heretics,
The idolatries, the druids, and
The end of wicked women.
As I preached the gospel,
There came Caoilte of the Fianna,
Who arrived with huge giants of men
As they approached,
I simply sprinkled them with holy water,
And the big men sat down,
I gave them food and drink,
All talked with them of the good news,
Angels appeared to protect me,
But I told Brogan the scribe
To write down the stories of these men,
And in parts of Ireland,
They are repeated and sung in song.

Brogan and I once heard
The spirit of tunes of Cas Corach.
He was a young man wearing a green cloak,
With a silver brooch
And a yellow silk shirt,
Covered over by a coat of soft satin.
Around his neck he carried a harp.
The singer told the story
Of dead heroes and great warriors,
Oh, how the Irish love to mourn
In a lively, long but doleful way.
There up on the green ground
On the Meadow of the Two Stags
Where the men of Weltse
Leading their descendants in the war
For the Bull of Cuailnge.
Let us hear your news and skill,
And he said:

VOICE:
I will do honor
To the plans of the apostle of the Irish.

PATRICK:
And soon we fell asleep
From the subtle sounds
And the ardors of the day.
What can I give you in return?
And Cas Corach responded,
"Heaven for myself, and good luck
For my art and those who follow."
If there is verse in the human heart
It is tunes like those.
Should heaven hear my mission
Or does God overwhelm the senses,
For the songs are worldly,
But are so beautiful.
I pushed in words to the Son,
And told the Irish of God,
Of the truly, co-equal persons,
Who had no beginning and no end.
He was the great Creator of all being,
I taught them the new Creed,
Told them of the Son and the Holy Spirit,
And of God's love and grace.

To preach the good news,
I had to pay bribes to Irish kings,
And the British bishops censured me.
A soul for a coin,
Is not a bad bargain.
The kings were like wild beasts,
And in some tribes they were gods.
"Molen, he is the only son of King Aine,
Like a god among gods."

The kings and their warriors cut off
The heads of their opponents,
And took Celtic trousers
Unlike our tunics.
The Druids told them,
I would overthrow their kingdoms,
Destroy the gods
And set up myself as king.
I built churches where they
Wished to kill a doe and a fawn.
I matched their darkness
With bright Irish light
From the risen Christ

Who takes all into the dawn.

They watched it with the King
Of Lungus, the inventor of arts
And a guide to cultic journeys.

Yet the Druids believed
In eternal life,
People were reincarnated
In new lives and bodies,
Some of their priests told
The frenzied Irish to move around them.
But I focused on young women there,
And they took baptism and celibacy together.

Across the island we roamed,
With a crosier in hand
And the Eucharist near our heart.

I had to oppose the Druids
And random kings of violence,
That I expected, but much worse
Was the opposition of British bishops,
Who accused me of subjecting Britons
To my Irish church, of bribes to kings
To support my lavish life…
I owned two tunics…
And they even reminded each other
In their gossip of my earliest great sin,
Which I never denied,
I was charged before them
Of corruption, but like Paul
I was selected to convert the Gentiles.
"To many, I am the most despised.
Listen, great and small,
God charged foolish little me
From all of you wise and expert
To preach to the Celtics,
And so I must go forward
To service the Irish people faithfully,
Laugh, and make fun of me if you wish,
I will not keep quiet,
Nor give up the sign,
The wonderful things
God has revealed.
I leave with your condemnation

In my ears and your censures at my work
To rescue my mission in Ireland
And I have earned only an unmarked
Nameless Christian grave."

VOICE:
Listen everyone, all you who love God,
To the qualities of blessed Patrick
The bishop who is like the holy angels
In his wonderful ways,
Equal to the apostles and their prayful lives.

When he came to die,
He walked slowly with his crozier
To Ard Mhacha, but Victor the angel
Stopped him and told him
To go to a certain barn,
"For there your death will be."
And for twelve nights,
The angels kept a respectful vigil,
The men of Ulster and Ua Neill fought over his body.
He told his disciples—

PATRICK:
"I Patrick, a sinner,
Have asked God's final forgiveness.
I have kept the faith,
Run the good race,
And loved the newly converted
Peoples of this Sacred Isle."

*The premier performance of this play was directed by Dr. Lawrence
McCullough at the Hamilton Stage for the Performing Arts in Rahway, N.J. St.
Patrick was played by Micheál Ó'Máille, famed Gaelic actor. At the end of the
play the audience made up of mainly parishioners of Divine Mercy parish,
originally an Irish-American parish, spontaneously rose and sang in Gaelic,
"Hail, Glorious St. Patrick." The lyrics are given here in English*

Hail, glorious St. Patrick, dear saint of our isle,
On us thy poor children bestow a sweet smile;
And now that you're high in your mansions above,
On Erin's green valleys look down with your love.

On Erin's green valleys, on Erin's green valleys,
On Erin's green valleys look down with your love.

Hail, glorious St. Patrick, thy words were once strong
Against Satan's wiles and a heretic throng;
Not less is thy might where in Heaven thou art;
Oh, come to our aid, in our battle take part!

In a war against sin, in the fight for the faith,
Dear Saint, may thy children resist to the death;
May their strength be in meekness, in penance, and prayer,
Their banner the Cross, which they glory to bear.

Thy people, now exiles on many a shore,
Shall love and revere thee till time be no more;
And the fire thou hast kindled shall ever burn bright,
Its warmth undiminished, undying its light.

God bless and defend the sweet land of our birth,
Where the shamrock still blooms as when thou wert on earth,
And our hearts shall yet burn, wherever we roam,
For God and St. Patrick, and our native home.

THE POOR MAN OF ASSISI

Dedicated to Rev. Richard P. Lewandowski

THE POOR MAN OF ASSISI

ACT I, SCENE 1
(in a jail)

JAILER:
Oink, oink, food time,
My dear Francesco, food time.
Don't ask for the extended menu,
Notice it is not in French!
It is the same as yesterday
And the day before,
And will be the same tomorrow
And a thousand tomorrows ahead.
Welcome to our jail
With dirty crusty windows
And rusty crossbar gates.
This is the luxury suite,
 Gallant young warrior.
This is what happens
When you go to war
Against mighty Perugia.

FRANCESCO:
Like all knights
In all the sterling lights
Of gallant songs of sweet Provence,
We welcome battle, even a quick death.
What is more heroic than to live and die
For the needs of a beautiful damsel?
(sings)
Oh, sweet lady, you hold my heart
In your dainty hands,
For I treasure your heart,
Treasure your luminous eyes,
Envy the slim form of a true noble lass.

JAILER:
In case, you are blind, boy,
There are no damsels in distress
Here, or damsels at all.
This is a rusted converted pigsty
And you are our oink.
You are only treated so well by me
Because my captain expects your father
To pay a fine ransom to buy you home.

FRANCESCO:
If the gold coins never come,
Then I shall start a career
As an Italian troubadour,
Singing while the sun is asleep,
And the moon is up.

JAILER:
Wait, wait!
Wait, wait!
Ah, he has come himself,
Your beloved father brings us
The gold coins to ransom you,
Great troubadour, if I were you
I would sing a song to rejoice.
I have treated you well,
Have I not, son of Pietro Bernardone?

FRANCESCO:
Better than the usual pig.

JAILER:
Then give me a token in return.
How about that gold cross
Around your thin scrawny neck?
You can buy another
In the stalls back in Assisi.
I am only a poor soldier
Living on a meager salary.

FRANCESCO: *(carefully takes off the gold cross)*
Wear it in good health,
I will think of you at my first welcome party.

PLENARY INDULGENCES

SCENE 2

FATHER:
Thank God, you are alive—
I wanted a man's man,
And am proud of your service
To our beloved, troubled city,
But war is for stronger cities and older men.
At 22, you need to be learning my trade,
And bring home a fertile wife to start a family.
I want a boy named after me,
For such is one of the few ways
We have dependable immortality on earth.

FRANCESCO:
I will give you what
You want when you need it.

FATHER:
Enjoy the weeks, go and rejoice again
With friends of lesser courage.
Pay their drinks as usual
With my hard-earned money,
Enjoy the pleasures of young women
And then their older, seasoned sisters.
You will soon come home
To start on a trip to France.
But first see mama.
She misses so your songs,
For she is also a lover of Provence.
Cantare, Francesco, Cantare.

FRANCESCO:
It is what I do best,
For though I am a warrior at heart,
I am not a warrior in arms anymore.
I am meant to sing of other
Great men's gallant deeds and sturdy captures.
God bless you, father, for your mercy—
You are my savior today as always.

SCENE 3
(Back in Assisi, A group of high spirited men arrive at an inn.)

GROUP 1:
We are fit to welcome Francesco,
To drink his wine with his father's money,
To sing the sweet songs of Provence
To the not so fresh women of this august temple.
Enough of war and the rancid things of war,
Violence only breeds more violence,
And is paid for with the blood of the young.

GROUP 2:
We will not fight till they call up
The council leaders and their effete sons,
Boys who are men and live in Rome,
Love in Paris, study in Bologna,
And let Assisi rot in hell.
(Enter FRANCESCO)

FRANCESCO:
War is a good, healthy exercise,
It is captivity that is hell.

GROUP 1:
How is a Perugian jail,
As rotten as its cheese,
As diluted as its wine?

FRANCESCO:
I had no cheese or wine,
Only daily gruel and dirty water.
I would rather be with you,
Aimless, unprincipled, and drunk.
At least it isn't damp here.
Throw another log on the fire,
And pass around the reddest wine
You have made without me.

GROUP 1:
At least, Assisi is the same.
The timid souls lost in meaning,
Making money, obeying God
Only on Sundays and Church holidays.
Our times are meant to produce
More merchants, more coin collectors,

More rich men's clothing.
We travel to the East
To buy from the rapacious Venetians,
And sell to happy Romans.

FRANCESCO:
There must be more in life,
My comrades, I know the selling trades,
Now I know the castrations of war,
Little seems to matter
To me, but you dearest friends.

GROUP 1:
And we are all believers in nothing.
Nothing matters in the end.
It is all il nulla.
For graves are dust by the roadsides,
And the beautiful nobles of our time
Buy rugs that dogs soon piss on.

FRANCESCO:
We need more meaning than that.
For surely a life that is so short
Should be marked by gentle beauties
Of all hues and types.

GROUP 2:
Yes, you have said it all.
One must mark our days
With wine and sad songs.
But in the end, the meaning of life
Is life itself. The rest is
Wind and rain and the moon,
Only a shining sun makes us feel good.

FRANCESCO:
Brother sun, sister moon…

GROUP 2:
They are not real, but moldy rocks
Placed far away from our soft hands.
Look at that bright light.
Way, way over there.
We are so far away,
And all we know for certainty,
Is we love to hate, and set fast

The emblems of our selves.

FRANCESCO:
Even pagans worshipped the sun.

GROUP 1:
They never knew anything else,
Ignorance is the foundation of all faith.
We walk our days in a daze.
When we are young we dreamed,
When in middle age we have addictions,
When we are old we have sad, vague memories.
And so it goes, one generation to another.
And then like velvet flowers we die,
Soon even our children do not know us,
Our grandchildren not at all.

FRANCESCO:
I once tried fame—

GROUP 1:
And it got you
In a cellar of heroes,
You are here only because
A generous father forgave you.
Without him you would pick up
Pig droppings day and night,
And call that noble work.

FRANCESCO:
I cannot live that way.
At 22, I am spent and soiled,
Prisoner in a sick ward.
I know I have paid for my errors.
(They eat and drink hardily)

SCENE 4

FATHER:
Wake up, my son,
Now you must pay for too much drink
With boys of no purpose or ambition.
Take this potion.
(FRANCESCO drinks and vomits up everything)
There is no other way to purge the body,

Would that it were so easy to purge the soul.
Look at this cloth,
It is beautiful, mother and I made it for you.
The clothier's son should have the best cloaks.
Get in the back of the cart.
We are going to Paris.

FRANCESCO:
Why Paris?

FATHER:
To buy the very best of styles,
And so you may learn how a great city
Moves aimlessly day by day.

FRANCESCO:
But should we go to Rome?

FATHER:
Rome is about the Church,
You learn nothing from celibates
Who have all the answers
Regardless of the questions.
In Paris, there are bedecked clothes
With sparking finery and golden jewels,
And women worthy to wear them.
Yes, you can hear new songs
From the romantic Provence poets—
The yearning for unreachable women,
The true ardor of mating girls
And their designing mothers,
Watch out for men who cheat you,
For in Paris there is much money.
And where there is much money,
There are thieves of all sorts.
You must become more
Alert to the deceiving world,
It is good in life to be trusting,
To be kind, to be sensitive,
But first I must toughen you up
Or the world will cheat you of your very tunic.
All we have is family,
And even then more members are
Absent, surly, involved,
Angry about something.
They don't even remember

What it was.
We say we serve revenge cold,
That is because we don't remember the wrongs.
Now you go down the anxious street of gold
And look for jewelry,
I will buy yards of novel designs.
(FRANCESCO is wide eyed and dazed)

SCENE 5
(Back in Assisi)

FATHER:
It was a good trip, Francesco?
A fruitful and money making voyage,
But what did you learn?

FRANCESCO:
Only what you told me, papa.
Merchants do not want to do business
With the young and impressionable.
They tried to overcharge me
And give me the worst of their wares.

FATHER:
Yes, yes it is so.
(Out comes mother)

MOTHER:
Thanks be to God you are here,
My boys, I needed you so.
I have worried everyday
About the bandits, the wild troops,
Who roam the rugged mountains
Who plague us so.

FATHER:
Here, be happy, your romantic son
Has heard new songs,
The type you love, dear.
The newest sounds of Provence.
Go inside and sing for her,
If you sing out here,
The animals will get scared.

SCENE 6
(In the woods)

FRANCESCO:
So I do need free time,
To walk the roads, touch the leaves,
Watch nature in all her garments.
We have two sacred scriptures:
The Bible and nature,
And we live in both of them.
My parents are so caring about me,
After jail all my mother worried about was how
To protect me from hostilities,
And papa knew what I did was right,
Said nothing, but as a loyal man
Works in that shop
From the dull morning to lonely night.
I will walk today as far
As I can, off the edge of the earth
To see what is at the frontier,
Is it really hell or a higher stage
Of a magnificent light of heaven.
What ends at the end?
Strange outlines but a different shape?
Why do those assorted animals seem
To get along well, while we men
Kill each other even if we look alike?
For what—merely flat land, or military posts,
Or living space, or wealth,
While most of us die at 40?
My life is half up.
Is it the good or the bad half gone?
I have eaten little since
I was found, and drank too much.
I cannot taste the differences
The spices, the salt, the sharp herbs.
They are the barren tastes
Of an old man eating with an old lady.
Yet I know in my heart of hearts
My body doesn't need the wine,
My mind sips it to kill
The haunting shocks at night,
And the strange daytime visions.
The wine is just like any other cover—
A thin blanket over my sick nothingness,
Il nulla, nulla.

It dulls the memory,
And the despair inside me.
I cannot see shapes of things,
But squares, triangles, cords
All meshed together,
And for what purpose?
What do I see is a clown,
A king of the revels, they call me.
Whether I succeed or fail,
I am still a clown,
Watch me twirl, see....
I am a dervish as in the East.
(He spins around like a top until he falls down dizzy.)
But I need to be a fool of God.
Leave me sit here, for the night
Is getting dark, and I am very weary,
Weary for no real reason.
(And he finally falls asleep.)
*(The night brings lightning and thunder, but no rain, and at daybreak
FRANCESCO wakes up shaking:)*

FRANCESCO:
He said to me, "Fix my church."
This old rundown structure.
It would be better to let it fall,
But he commanded,
"Fix my church, Francesco,
You will be connected to Me forever,
If you fix my church."
Instead of worrying about this structure,
You might fix your Holy Roman Church in Rome.
It is rotten to the core.
Ah, sometimes it is best not to be
Too smart by half, "Fix the church."
I must get the pastor's permission to do it.
Hopefully he will deny me permission...

But he did not do that.
It was like he knew I was coming.
So I sold all I had
To buy timbers and nails,
All on my father's account.
But no one helped me,
And I am a merchant,
My hands are soft,
And the work was long.

I needed my friends' help,
But they abandoned me once
I was not a drinking host.
Some must sell their family farms,
Come and help me,
And God will prove it was love.
…And then, my father came.

FATHER:
Enough, nonsense,
Get up and return home,
And let us start again at my shop.

FRANCESCO:
I can't turn that into a calling.

FATHER:
Who is talking of a calling?
It is a way of living:
To make money, put food on the table,
And pay your drinking bills.
My son, come back.

FRANCESCO:
I am giving my life to Christ,

FATHER:
Then we will talk to the bishop,
He owes me much,
And see if we can get you a steady position.
No one gets to the top in the Church
Starting at the bottom.

SCENE 7

(In the town plaza, Francesco appears wearing a golden tunic and a chained necklace from his father's shop. In the plaza people are gathering. His father and mother are standing near the bishop of Assisi. FRANCESCO moves toward middle stage. They are on the right.)

FRANCESCO:
Loyal bishop, heir of Christ's apostles,
Hear my humble public petition.
I am now called by God
To plead with you to accept me
In a lay brotherhood of the Church,

To let me walk away from all love
On earth to become a poor begging friar,
And to teach God's mercy.
I wish to beg for my food,
Live in a cave,
Be poor beyond belief,
Preach to all who will listen,
Or even wonder about the good news.
(Points to the church buildings)
I do not wish
The church to support me,
Or to take me into the rectory.
This is not simple enough,
For you are a prince of the church,
And I am a knave of the Lord.
I want to live like Christ Jesus lived,
Live, without honors,
Live without money, or fame,
Or even a devoted family.

FATHER:
(Speaking to the bishop.)
That is easy to say,
For 24 years I have supported him,
Paid his bills, ransomed him,
And now he abandons
The reputation of his caring family.

FRANCESCO:
Jesus said we must give up
Father, mother, sisters, brothers,
And donate all our riches to God.

BISHOP:
My dear Francesco,
You are taking too literally
The sacred words of Scripture.
Jesus stayed at times in Peter's house,
Cured his mother-in-law with His own hands,
Loved the meals of Martha and Mary,
Had the whore bathe his feet
With expensive perfumes and imported oils.
Jesus spoke to mortal men
On different levels—sons of the harsh world,
Sons bothered in their deep hearts,
Sons capable of special spiritual insights.

Work for Christ, by doing it
In a more moderate way.

FRANCESCO:
This is what He told me
In the secret of the night.
He said to give up my father on earth
To tell me to come to Him.

MOTHER:
Francesco, please come home
To your father and me.
We have waited
So long for you to be home.
To free you from your jailer
And live a quiet life with us.

FRANCESCO *(in a bolt of fury)*:
I have no father but God,
Here take all my clothes,
My jewels, even my sandals,
Now I have no father on earth,
My only father is in heaven
(Bishop rushes to throw a blanket over his naked body, and gives him his own braided belt for a waist band.)

FRANCESCO:
They fear a naked man,
But God makes us naked,
And naked we will leave.
Now I will beg from the world,
I will depend on its good will
And God's hidden pleasure.
(His old friends start throwing rocks and mud at him.)

FATHER: *(Quietly)*
Mother, have some serving girls,
He does not know, give him food
Without his notice of it.
(Crowd dissipates, and then all that is left is a disheveled Francesco. People are screaming, "He is here again, kill him, get your clubs, we have him cornered." FRANCESCO thinks they mean him.)

FRANCESCO:
Are you afraid of the poor man of Assisi?

CROWD:
No, it is the wolf of Gubbio,
He is back again, killing our sheep.
Carrying our babies away.
We will surround and kill him once and for all.

FRANCESCO:
Wait, let me talk to him.
(and he moves toward left
And sees the vicious wolf)
Brother Wolf, why do you attack
Our people and their animals?
You scare these children,
And now they wish to kill you.
Remember it well, that you
Like me are a creature of God.
Come here first,
I was a merchant's son,
I know how to make a contract.
If you promise not to attack,
I will see these people feed you
Every day, and then you can walk free,
Without fear, playing with the children
Who think you are only a large dog.
(Wolf puts his paw on FRANCESCO'S right hand)
So be it. Let me introduce you
To the people of this city.
Look they are our friends,
Brother Wolf has given me his promise
And at night we will feed him at the church door
Where you leave him food and water,
He will protect you
And yours from attacks on the city.
Now I myself must find food,
I will return,
Without a Bible,
Or any possessions.
God bless this wolf,
Brother sun is down,
And the days are too long
For work or even calm church programs.
Shake my hand, again.
Stay faithful, Brother Wolf.

ACT II, SCENE 1

FRANCESCO:
We must all begin to beg,
For our food, our drink, and our salvation.
But I remain a troubadour,
This time I sing to Lady Poverty.
Dear Lady, you prevent my distractions
To the ways and wiles of the world.
I can mull over the crucifixion of Christ,
The terrible wounds of our Savior,
The way that a God who is a man feels,
And I cry, I cry so hard that I have
Lines from my tears,
And my eyes grow dim,
For eyes are meant to express joy,
Sweet long lasting wonder,
The experience of nature, look about you,
And every morn say, "Gratis Deo,"
Thanks be that I am alive
To do praise to You
And all the fruits of Your labor.
I still cry when I see in my mind
The terrible wounds of the cross
While you died for me.
For I am a man who is a sinner,
But who like the hypocrites in the temple,
Preaches salvation and good works for others.
(Approached by a noble man, Bernardo)

BERNARDO:
I have watched you from afar
For some time, what is it you sell?

FRANCESCO:
I sell salvation, do you want to buy?
You have a cloak that will last a few years,
Sandals that will fray in months,
Jewels that glisten, but are easily stolen.
I promise you salvation
For all eternity, and you have either
To put them away or clean them,
Or keep an eye on the servants
Who are prone to steal.
Salvation is a contract

Between God and you.
Come, follow me.

BERNARDO:
I am planning to go to war,
To achieve fame and fortune,
I cannot follow you and follow the troops too.
This is what I was made for.

FRANCESCO:
You were made in God's image.
And He is not a warrior king,
He is not a wealthy merchant,
He is not a God of war, but of love.

BERNARDO:
But I do not even know Him,
I haven't seen Him, or touched Him,
Or even served His confusing causes.
War is what I am made for.

FRANCESCO:
No, I thought so too.
Pray with me:
"Lord,
Make me an instrument of your peace.
Where there is hatred, let me bring love.
Where there is injury, let me bring pardon.
Where there is discord, let me bring union.
Where there is error, let me bring truth.
Where there is doubt, let me bring faith.
Where there is despair, let me bring hope.
Where there is darkness, let me bring light.
And where there is sadness, let me bring joy.
Divine Master, grant that
I may not so much seek
To be consoled as to console,
To be understood as to understand,
To be loved as to love,
For it is in giving that we receive,
It is in self-forgetting that one finds,
It is in pardoning that we are pardoned,
And it in dying that we are born to eternal life."
That is what it is all about.
Sell what you have
Give it to the poor,

Come then and follow me,
For in doing so you are following Him
And the commission will last forever.
(BERNARDO leaves to sell all he has)
So this is how it goes:
One soul at a time, one soul for Christ.
Now I need to find more friars,
We shall beg together,
And tell the world of the new gospel
Which they knew in their hearts
All their lives but did not live it.
(As he sits there he has begun to make a small Nativity scene with twigs and hay, and primitive wooden figures. This is to celebrate the birth of the Savior in Bethlehem.)
A barn made of sticks and straw,
And figures children carve,
But we are all the Lord's family,
As we are all our own family.
This order will teach this
Lesson to everyone they visit.
(As he roams around stage, he is slowly joined by other men with brown tunics and sandals, then he sees a young woman looking at them.)

CLARE:
Salvation is not just for men,
This is not war or playing ball,
Francesco, what of the other half
Of God's creation, what of the women?

FRANCESCO:
They can pray for the men,
Provide them with food and drink,
Be mothers to us all.

CLARE:
That is not enough, Francesco,
I want to attract women
To serve the same mission,
To live in poverty,
To show by our example
That we accept your gospel.
We know the Church will not allow
Us to preach,
Although we did with the apostle Paul.
But this is not a lenient Church for women.
Take us into your churches, your order, and your prayers.

Do you have a rule against it?
Has God told you to exclude
One half of the human race?

FRANCESCO:
No, He has never mentioned it.
He simply said, "Follow Me.
Fix up my church,
Sell all you have, live a life
Of mercy and compassion."

CLARE:
I am fortunate to come
From a noble family near this site,
So I can indeed sell
What I have been given,
And parcel it to the poor,
The unfortunate, the most vulnerable,
Just as I hear that you were once young,
And gave away your possessions.
Now you must remember the ladies.

FRANCESCO:
I have not thought that way,
I can't have your ladies live with us,
For we have enough temptations
In that way already,
For my friars are young and virile men,
And pray ardently for chastity,
But the mind is ungovernable.
Go, daughter Clare,
Go found a new order, a second
Devoted to good ladies,
Who will live a life of poverty and prayer.
Pray for me, good sister.

CLARE:
Give me your blessing,
Beloved friar, so I can bring it back.
(He moves forward and quietly cuts her long hair.)

FRANCESCO:
No, together we must kneel
And pray for His blessing,
For our yoke is sweet,
Our burden is light.

(She leaves, and behind him is the bishop of Assisi.)

BISHOP:
That was a bad mistake, my son.
She is only 18 and innocent.
She will never beg enough
To feed her order,
And will be back to you and to me
For food and shelter,
And who can say no to beautiful women?
You have set up a competition
With yourself and your new group.
You need to create a rule like Benedict did,
So your order as it grows
Has some sacred rules, for disputes
Are in the nature of things,
Especially with men in religious orders,
They have little else but disputes,
Gossip, and a search for rank.

FRANCESCO:
Well, then give us such a rule.

BISHOP:
No, not I, a new order must come
From the Holy Father's hands,
From Innocent III.
Go to Rome, and plead with him.
He has spies all over the land,
He knows what you are doing,
And since he has not stopped it,
He must agree in some way.
He is a rigorous, but fair man,
He is a king above kings,
It would be good for him
In his majestic palace to meet you
And your motley group,
For even diamonds start out as coal.

SCENE 2
(At the papal court of Innocent III, the most powerful pontiff in history who assumed office at 32 years old.)

Singing in the background the Te Deum:
"Oh God, we praise Thee, and

Acknowledge Thee to be the supreme Lord.
Everlasting Father, all the earth worships Thee
All the Angels, the heavens, and all angelic powers.
All the cherubim and seraphim, continuously cry to Thee
Holy, Holy, Holy, Lord of Hosts!"
(The hymn continues on as the procession fades away, and INNOCENT and the
BISHOP are left alone.)

INNOCENT:
I do love that hymn,
Only Ambrose could write
Such a fine harmony,
That links music and theology.
(Pope hums:)
"Te Deum laudamus te Dominum confitemur
To aeternum Patrem omnis terra venerator.
Tibi omnes Angeli; tibi caeli et universae Potestates….."
Ah, now we must get about the business of the day
People care little if their pope can sing,
They want him to pass the papers and decrees,
To solve their problems, to host their events.
Did you ever know a clerk who went to heaven?
Bishop, bring in this beggar from Assisi,
(In comes FRANCESCO and his troupe. They have walked to Rome and are
filthy.)

FRANCESCO:
Your holiness, we are honored to be here,
We come in the name of Christ Jesus,
To live as He did, to teach what He gave us.

INNOCENT:
Does the Church not do that?
Do we really need another order in the Church?
We have so many, cannot you join
The Benedictines or the hermits of Africa?
They have already their own rule.

BISHOP:
Your holiness these men are different.
They have given up their riches,
They have forsaken their education,
They even gave away their own Bible
To a poor roaming leper.

INNOCENT:
Could he even read it?
That is why we have stained glass windows
So the times of Jesus can be seen and understood
By those who are unlettered but pious.

BISHOP:
Holiness, Jesus told the rich men
To give away all and follow Him.
The noble man in the Scriptures could not do that then,
Now these honorable men,
Many of noble background do it.
Let Francesco of Assisi tell you
Their story, their narrative of sacrifice.

INNOCENT:
(Sarcastically)
You are filthy, you should first preach
To the pigs outside the basilica,
Roll around with them,
And tell them the good news.

FRANCESCO:
(without any protest)
We shall go right now,
And preach to brother pig,
Come my brothers. *(They exit).*

BISHOP:
He is a good man,
More importantly he is a holy man,
This Church cannot afford to lose him,
Thousands are now following him,
In so many ways, it is like a daily
Sermon on the Mount.

INNOCENT:
Give me a day to think about it.
I now have another friar,
A Dominic, who wishes a new order
That stresses high intelligence and preaching.
Which is the future of the Church?
Bishop, what would you do?

BISHOP:
You are by training a lawyer,

You know that any well run state
Has many different types of laws,
For many different types of people.
More people pray the faith,
Than read about it in theology.
(Exit quietly, INNOCENT and BISHOP.)

SCENE 3

FRANCESCO:
I do not know if the pigs understood,
But we obeyed the Holy Pontiff,
And washed up a little by the Tiber.

BISHOP *(enters):*
Francesco, say little this time,
Let him just see your humility,
And trust the Holy Spirit to inspire.
For he is a good man
With many worries.

INNOCENT:
Ah, my friends, how were the pigs?
They are useful in their own way,
But I doubt there are too many souls there!
Last night, my son, I had a powerful dream,
In the deepest part of the night,
I saw my Church crumbling,
And only you and your friars
Could hold it up.
Not my efforts, or my bishops,
Or my prayers, nor all the *Te Deums*
In the wide world made a difference.
I saw a palm tree growing
Up between my legs at night.
I must assume that God
Is telling me to let you be.
I will grant you a rule for five years,
And then I will review it.
If your order works,
Maybe I will resign and join!
Many kings and cardinals would welcome that.
Go in peace, and take my blessing.
Francesco, here is my personal Bible.
Take it, read it, but do not sell it,
And do not give it away.

It is a personal gift from me to you.

ACT III, SCENE 1

FRANCESCO: *(on the road back to Assisi)*
We now have a charter for the order,
The pope himself has certified it.

BERNARDO:
But we do not have a charter,
Only his words that were tentative,
We need to stress that we
Have only five years to show
That we can establish a friars group
Dedicated to God and to Lady Poverty.

FRANCESCO:
We shall act as if I have the charter
In my tunic, protecting it from the elements.
It is better to suffer chastisement
Than to seek permission.
Go, and tell Clare that the order
Covers her and her young ladies,
For they are even more devoted
To God and poverty than we.
We have covered all the peninsula
From the Alps to Sicily
In so short a time.
Now I wish to go to Arabia,
Talk to the Mohammedans,
End the crusades, and convert them.
Call the band together,
This will be our greatest conquest.

BERNARDO:
That is a bad errand, my friend,
For many have tried and been killed.
The Arabs have their own god, and their own customs.
They believe in Allah, and are sure
That Jesus is just another fine prophet,
But not the Son of their God,
For Allah has no son or daughter,
But only one prophet, Mohammed.

FRANCESCO:
They do not know Christ Jesus,
No one has taken the time,

Given the effort to speak of Him,
For if they truly knew,
They would fall to their knees
And praise Him by another name.

BERNARDO:
They are fierce, roaming tribes,
Even Mohammed was challenged
And nearly beheaded.
We could not cover all that desert
By ourselves, without much water.
In these woolen robes.
Let it be.

FRANCESCO:
No, we cannot convert every Bedouin,
But we can convert the great Sultan of Egypt
For we are now near Sicily
And boats are plentiful.
The Sultan will order
That his tribes will follow our faith,
For we have been commissioned
By God himself to search the world,
To preach the good news of His reign,
And then we will baptize them
In all the splendor that is Christianity.
(Lights out)

SCENE 2

FRANCESCO:
Did you ever watch the birds?
They speak their own languages,
I wonder if they talk of us,
As we talk of them.
Come here, my brothers and sisters,
(To the birds)
God feeds you, gives you
Valleys and mountains for refuge,
Tall trees for your nests,
And you neither sow nor reap,
But your clothes are a marvel.
Let us confide in how you
Make nests and shelters,
Working together in harmony,
Meeting at the streams

As if you were in gossip
About the coming day.
(Turns to other friars)
Do you think that they go
To heaven, for if heaven is a place of joy
Then those of us who love these animals
Need them with us to serve the Lord.
I have come to see that it is joy
That is the center of our lives
Here on this sad earth,
Joy is alive, warm, pleasing,
And allows us to say, "Thanks be to God"
For the coming day and night.
They tell me that the devil owns the night,
But in the dark I pray for you and the world,
I see the marks of the cross and the piercing
Thorns of the bloody crown.
I can feel them in me and measure out
My life in drops of His blood.
I am a sinner, Lord, I know,
But I come to you on bended knee.

BERNARDO:
What is that on your hands?
Why are they wrapped up so?
Oh, My God, you have the marks
Of the cross on your hands…
And on your feet.
How can you walk?
Sit here, gather around friars.
Let us make him a pallet
And bear him in our arms.

FRANCESCO:
No, no, tell no one of these.
They are our secrets,
A contract between God
And a sinful merchant's son.

BERNARDO:
I have never seen these before
On the holiest of men.
What is it meant to tell us?

FRANCESCO:
That Christ bled like all mortal men,

And that I imitate His sacrifice
In some small insignificant ways.
(Suddenly, they are arrested by tribesmen)

FRANCESCO:
Brothers, I have come to see your Sultan,
Bring us to him.
(they stare at him)
Bring us to your Sultan,
Do any of you brothers know
Their tongue. *(One friar steps forward)*
Speak to them, Brother Illuminatus.

ILLUMINATUS:
They say no one sees the Sultan,
And he has give one Byzantine gold piece
For each Christian head.
Oh God!
He does though accept visitors
On the third day of the week
When he hears petitions.

FRANCESCO:
Tell them I have a petition
From the great king of Rome,
I come in peace
To present it to him and to his court.
(They drag the friars to the court)

SCENE 3

SULTAN: *(sitting in a large elegant tent)*
It is that time of the week
When I must hear the petitions
Of the weak, and the requests of the strong.
I do wish that people could do right,
By themselves, rule themselves, pray themselves.
Bring forth my people,
Let them see their Sultan this morning.
(Guards drag in FRANCESCO and his fellow friars)
Who are these strange people,
For surely they are not from Arabia?
Why are you here on the very day
I listen only to my people?

FRANCESCO:
Illuminatus, please translate to him:
That I bring from the great prince of Rome
The good news that God will save him
For all eternity, he will know more joy,
More mercy, more love than ever before.

SULTAN:
What is this nonsense?
We have Allah and we have Mohammed,
What do we need from this prince of Rome?
All those allies of his bring us is death and destruction,
What type of good news is that?
Who is this man?

ILLUMINATUS:
He wants to know who you are,
And why should he trust the leader of
The blood thirsty crusaders.
We have obviously chosen a bad time
To make our entrance.

FRANCESCO:
See clearly, honorable king,
We are not warriors or crusaders,
But humble men before a great Sultan.
We bring you the good news that God
Died for your sins, and now you can be
Assured that He will come again to judge
All, and the Sultan will never be overthrown,
Or defeated by enemies.
For if you give us the Arabs
We will assure you that you will be
A saint in our heaven.

SULTAN:
I have been told I will go to heaven
To the land of our prophets,
Surrounded by 72 virgins,
And seeing Allah in all his glory.
Can you do better?
Why don't you convert to Islam,
For surely your men could use some virgins,
To save them from the frights of the night.
Even with my many wives, I still feel it.
Suppose great teacher, I give you several of my wives

For tonight, and then in the morning we can talk of God.

FRANCESCO:
I would enjoy talking with you more,
But we are celibate and women would
Distract us from our gospel.

SULTAN:
That is a sad gospel,
For you say you are full of joy,
But women are the core of joy
On earth, and we believe in heaven.
Even I cannot service 72 beauties
With almond colored eyes.
But as you will,
Tomorrow then?
(FRANCESCO and the friars leave)
This thin man is different
From anyone in the kingdoms,
But he speaks so sincerely
That I believe that he has some blessings
To impart on me and my tribes.
There are so many ways to Allah,
I wonder if there is simply one Allah,
And many paths to him,
Or if he is just a figment of our minds,
And none of us are right.
May Allah forgive my doubt.

SCENE 4

FRANCESCO: *(enters court)*
Great leader, I come to you
In humility, knowing too well
I cannot give you any reasons
Why you should change.
It is in your heart that change lies.
Are you willing to praise Christ Jesus,
And tell your kingdom that they will
Find true salvation with us?

SULTAN:
I have thought all night
And I believe in my ignorant heart,
That you are right,

But I cannot tell my people
To give up what they know,
What their sons die for,
What their fathers believed,
Based on your word and my feelings.
Go in peace, my little friend,
You may travel all over Arabia with my protection,
Here take my cloak and let all know
That you are my ward.

FRANCESCO:
Think of me, my lord,
For when you come to the end,
Pray to the God of the poor man of Assisi,
I have little in goods to give,
But take my cross and hold it dear.
For remember, the kingdom is at hand.

SULTAN:
You are a great teacher,
Little man, go with Allah,
And I will give you this horn
To call men to pray.
We kneel down to Mecca
Five times every day.

FRANCESCO:
A fine custom worthy
Of devout Christians too.

SULTAN:
Go home and tell your Crusaders
That you met with the madman Sultan of Egypt
Related to Suleiman the Magnificent,
And he loved you too.

SCENE 5

BERNARDO:
We should put you on a donkey,
So our travels are not so painful to you.
For it is a long way to the boat,
And even longer to feel the confines of home.

FRANCESCO:
No I am fine,
I am just a little bloody
From the old wounds,
It is fine.

BERNARDO:
No, we all insist,
You cannot be a leader,
If you are not a good follower.
(Puts his hand on FRANCESCO 's brow)
Your head is burning,
And your eyes look so weary
You cannot see the nature
You so love. It is the sand.
It is the failures that you have faced.
Even Jesus did not reach all with
The measures of success and triumph.
For woe brings woe.
You have taught us humility,
Now we must teach you
How to take care of yourself.
Here, eat more.
It is a sin to abstain from God's food.
Do it slowly, and as we walk
We will pray for you.

FRANCESCO:
If I eat as you wish,
I would be giving up my beliefs,
For poverty and hunger
Go together. How can I
Tell you to fast and abstain,
And then eat because I am sick.

BERNARDO:
Without food, you will die,
And who will ever hear of
Francesco and his gospel?
We have friars and friends all over the
Peninsula but without you, they will
Vanish like water under the Umbrian sun.
Eat and sit quietly on this donkey.

SCENE 6
(Clare's nunnery)

SISTER:
He is here, he is here!
A message from Francesco,
He says that the pope himself
Has granted the order
By special papal blessing.
We are now official in the eyes of the Church,
Your work has paid off.

CLARE:
God be praised,
Francesco is to be praised.
I knew in my heart he would
Bring us to the Promised Land,
But where Moses never lived,
To see his labors bear fruit,
We can view all the work worth the effort.

SISTER:
You too have a place in history,
All over Christian Europe.
Women have been inspired
In God's holy name
To follow your sanctified example.

CLARE:
I just followed Francesco,
And prayed to God I was right.
I was born a rich lady,
Betrothed to a knight,
Blessed with money and with hope,
But one day, I heard
Francesco speak of God's treasuries
And how we win immortality.
My father like his father
Was angry at us,
For we were children of privilege.
I could have been a noble lady,
A pampered wife, a doting mother,
But I gave it up to follow
Francesco and his strange ways.
His sermons were beautiful,
But as he spoke

He jumped around,
Flaying his thin arms,
And dancing with his flat feet,
We thought at first he was mad,
A fool for God in spite of himself.
A fanatic carrying religion
As a camp follower for foolish heroes.
But the words gushed forth
Like God's own enticement,
And all believed that what he said
Was a true and good inspiration.
Did the messenger tell you
What is the health of Francesco?

SISTER:
Not good at all,
He is propped up on a donkey,
To make his long trip easier,
And he can barely see
The wonders of nature he so loves.
He refuses to eat and drink
More than the most modest monk
Will take in a week.
He lives with stomach pains,
Grows irritable from it all
And most extraordinary,
He is a prisoner in his body.
His body was once freed by his father,
Now the words of the Savior must free him.
The bleeding is endless,
And he becomes weaker,
Especially as he does not eat meat
To rebuilt his emancipated body.
He is a captive in his own body,
The way he was a captive in Perugia.

CLARE:
But then his father rescued him,
Now only the Redeemer can free him.
His soul lives in a wasted body.

SISTER:
At times, his brothers feel
He wishes death to come,
He even calls it Sister Death.
The sick only get better

By will, and passion, and hope.
He welcomes sickness,
And then he became decrepit
For the sake of Christ Jesus.
He believes his work is done
And the order must plow
New ground and grow new crops
Of younger able friars.
But he insists on poverty so harsh,
Men fear to join his group.
He chastised the learned of the order
As if knowledge is an enemy of faith.

CLARE:
Francesco is so focused
On a life of poverty and simplicity,
Such is how we must be
For the good of the order.
Our bishop wishes us to become Benedictines,
But we are not moderate,
We are daughters of Francesco,
Ladies of the Second Order.

SISTER:
You should go to him.

CLARE:
When he arrives in Assisi,

SISTER:
No, he is stopping at Perugia,
For the pope is there
For a Church convention
And Francesco wishes to pay homage
To the vicar of St. Peter
Even though he is not in good shape.

CLARE:
Yes. I will go to Perugia
Oddly it is there he was in jail,
Now he will arrive in triumph
God is so mysterious and strange.

SCENE 7

(FRANCESCO and monks enter Perugia and find that the pope has come to the city, and then suddenly died)

ILLUMINATUS:
Francesco, the pope had come here
Maybe to look at us,
But God has taken him into heaven
So abruptly and without cause.
He was laid out in beautiful vestments
In the cathedral waiting for the cardinals.
But last night he was robbed of all his robes,
All his jewels, all his sacred vessels.

FRANCESCO:
The pope is dead, and now insulted,
The pope has been so good to us,
Let me off, I wish to go inside,
(and there he sees the pope stripped naked of all his vestments)
Oh my Lord, how could this happen?
(And he takes off his robe and wraps it around Innocent)
There, my Holiness, take my cloak,
For now as you said,
You are a follower of the order
You yourself made it happen.
(He leaves and is stopped by a leper and is given a small tunic for his naked body.)
So it has come to this,
A gift from my brother lepers,
You have scars on your body,
And I have them on my immortal soul.
You look strange and familiar,
Have I not seen you before in my prayers.
(The monks put him back on the donkey. He is delirious.)
Please no palms now,
No more sacrifices in the garden,
I bleed even more for your sins,
And yes, my eyes are so blurred.
If the eyes are the mirrors to the soul,
My soul is dark, and harsh,
And nasty to the world.
(BERNARDO leads him back to nearby hut near the cathedral. FRANCESCO also starts to pray, "My God, My God.")

SCENE 8
(In Assisi, FRANCESCO praying alone.)

STRANGER:
He will not come, friar,
For he knows you are a sinner,
And a hypocrite in a poor man's dress.
Were you not happy in the inn,
Were you not happy in the Perugian jail.
If life should be full of joy,
As you so often preach,
Where are you joyful?
You are a sad sack of a man,
And all your Gospel says so,
All your concerted efforts
Do not equal one moment of happiness.
Give me your soul, and I promise
You real joy and genuine pleasure.
Your temperature will break,
Your eyes sparkle,
Your appetite grow full.
You have starved yourself for what?
Enjoy the gifts of the earth,
Treasure others' company,
Give up the glories of poverty,
For they will lead nowhere,
Nothing, no place, no future.
Give me your soul,
I can surely do better
Than you have.
Look at your pope,
He is stripped of his shirt,
Even he foresaw he would
Never be let into heaven,
For power prevents holiness.
If he is unsafe,
Do you finally believe
You are safe and secure?
Come with me, Francesco,
It is time to give up
Early morning fasts,
And late night mortifications,
God created pleasures,
Even wild and gross ones,
So then enjoy them to the hilt.

FRANCESCO:
Get behind me, Satan,
For I am dedicated
To the life of the Savior,
You could not move me.

SATAN:
Damnable fool.

FRANCESCO:
See here, my words
(SATAN vanishes.)
Can I say the end of my Provencal,
"The sweet times of my first call,
Now chase Lady Poverty,
Sun and moon and God's property.
I love what I can see.
Let me come and suffer to be
The first form of the day.
Holy God's Mother in all the ways."
Oh God, forgive my singing
And into Your hands
I commend my spirit.

SCENE 9

(Later FRANCESCO is very sick and lying in a thatched hut. He has malaria, and his eyes are totally covered with a haze. He begins a long prayer, and then asks the friars to come in one at a time for his final legacy to them. In walks Clare as well, and she touches his wounds.)

CLARE:
He told me that he had them,
I did not believe it,
For these are the wounds of Christ,
No one has ever had these before.
Rest in peace, good man.

SCENE 10

BISHOP: *(to BERNARDO and ELIAS)*
And here he will be buried
Up on that hill, and there
We will build the church that
Will bring legions of admirers
To see the saintly Francesco.

Under the basement floor he will be buried,
On the top an elegant cathedral
Will be raised to praise God,
We will use gold and silver,
We will find the finished marble stone from Carrara,
And popes will come to pray,
Knowing that they will never be loved
As this poor man of Assisi.

BERNARDO:
Gold, silver, churches,
All we need are dancing girls.

ELIAS:
He never enjoyed pomp or display,
This would go against his whole life.
He wanted simplicity, poverty,
Love of the poor, the sick,
The lepers of life.

BISHOP:
Indeed, he did,
But now he belongs to posterity.

ST. CLARE OF ASSISI

To the women of the world
Who know suffering.

ST. CLARE OF ASSISI

ACT I, SCENE 1

CHORUS: *(invisible)*
If contempt of the world
Pleases you more than its hours,
Poverty more than those temporal riches,
And storing up treasures in heaven
Than on earth
You will be rewarded in heaven.
For heaven's treasure is not consumed
By rust, or rot, or destroyed by moths,
Or stolen by the boldest thieves,
And you will be called
The Savior's spouse, and bride
Of the Son of the Most High Father
And the glorious blessed Virgin Mary.

CLARE:
Oh, mother tell me again,
Tell me of your visit to the Holy Land.
I wish to walk with you,
To visit the garden Jesus
Prayed in as He contemplated
His horrid, coming crucifixion.
I want to fly from here to there,
To be lifted by any inspiration.
To walk the roads Jesus used.
To feel the Roman cobblestones,
Under my little feet
And stroke the very cross,
Bloody with the edge of His hand.
Let me dream with you.

MOTHER:
I do not know what more I can say.

You need to feel, think,
Smell the crucified men.
I went with you inside me.
On my first and only pilgrimage
To the Holy Land.

CLARE:
I wish to be you!

MOTHER:
No, I would be you!
In the Holy Land, the physicians told me
You would be great.
You would be able
To gaze at the crucified One
And see Jesus in person.
With your golden hair
And pretty form you will make
A fine mate for a young count.
When you were born your father
Arranged your marriage,
Rest assured you will inherit from God,
A good life, rather than the opposite,
And will pray joyfully for the future.

CLARE:
There surely are other ways
To live one's life than marriage...

MOTHER:
It is lonely being born to rule,
My husband is so proud of you,
But he is rarely around,
You feel like a camp follower
Waiting for his brief returns.

CLARE:
No one I know
Is so fortunate as you,
You are respected by all,
By your friends and opponents.
The mirror image is nearly cracked
By the forces of evil always around,
And we must see all that
Before it is too late to defend oneself.

MOTHER:
Thus men come and go,
Taking on crusades and splendid causes
And what do they bring us—
These wounded boys,
Sons of vagabonds and deep discontented spirits?
We have all heard their sayings and stories,
And they carry little,
But a few fine moments of melancholy
And unrequited love.
We seem never to get over
The legends of King Arthur,
All those men wished to have been
Lancelot, and all us Guinevere,
But they were adulterers,
And the king they swore to serve
Went to his death with visions
Of his ungrateful friends,
Each breaking their vows.

CLARE:
Life is not to be a love pact,
But the Godly poverty of the spirit
That is a favored power of the fortunate few.
I know not its origin,
But I can feel its intimate power
More than we possess.

MOTHER:
This is what there is,
It cannot be transformed,
You cannot elect the design later
Or cut off the tree tops to see the sun.
We must not be followers
Only carriers of ourselves.

CLARE:
Sometimes I am sure
We live on different floors
Of a building that has many levels.
And we can arise up only
With effort or with prayer.

MOTHER:
Your children and their children,
Will enjoy patiently your house

And pray for their father's return.
As for other worlds,
We can sit here
And live close by.

CLARE:
Most will be warriors
Who can tell us
Other visions and other plans,
While we can exist
In the brief collars of our days.
This surely cannot be all,
This surely cannot be for me.

MOTHER:
Girls would be enamored
Of your golden locks just as men are.
They belong to a young queen,
Like a youthful Guinevere.

CLARE:
Thank you so much…,
Now tell me again of Jerusalem.

MOTHER:
You were in me,
And I traveled only by coach and boat.
The roads were harsh Roman stones
And at the center of the sacred city
Were the remains of the collapse
Of the temple with not one rock
Laying on one another, as Jesus predicted.
I walked up slowly
The street of sorrows,
Walked in the footsteps of Christ.
At the beginning of the walkway
There was an ancient building
That had a handprint in the rock,
Not chiseled in,
But laid in an irregular way,
It was the palm print
Of the weary Christ on his way up.

CLARE:
Oh, how marvelous
What did it look like?

MOTHER:
It was a palm print
In the sandstone,
It is hard to describe it beyond that.
At the end of the Street of Sorrows
Is the site of the Crucifixion,
But instead of calm and quiet,
The monks of different faiths
Argue and chatter and sell
Olive bead rosaries,
All of which they claim from Bethlehem.

CLARE:
Are they, mother, are they?

MOTHER:
Who knows, but I bought several.
In the Holy Sepulcher,
I touched the spot
Where Our Lord was buried
And where the sacred cross was inserted.
Then we went to the Last Supper site,
A large room above the tomb of King David,
Or so they say,
We also viewed the quiet plains
Where Jesus recited the beatitudes,
The keys to the kingdom of God:
Blessed are the meek, and the poor,
The peacemakers, the good of heart.
Right on that spot
The gospels say He preached,
And men and women listened
And now we remember the words,
Which inform our hardened heart,
And all the listeners are gone.

CLARE:
And there He taught us to say
The paternoster, the one prayer
God the Son said to the Father,
And we say it every day in humility.

MOTHER:
I hope after you marry the young count
You two can go to see the Holy Land.
It is a desert that blooms regularly,

The spots where the Christians,
The Jews and the new Arabs
Come to worship an unnameable God.

CLARE:
What does it feel like,
Smell like, sound like, and taste like
As one sits there alone?

MOTHER:
Ah, Clare, you are too much
A child of the senses.
The Holy Land is simply
A blessed place where He was born,
Preached, died, and resurrected.
There it was just a dessert,
Desperately in need of cool water,
Day after day,
Night after night.
You will see,
I hope very soon.
Let it be our bridal gift for you.

CLARE:
Mother, I am too young.

MOTHER:
Old enough,
Let us go.
Soon your father will be back
From the wars, full of tales
Of high adventure and low intrigue.
Carrying relics and jewels,
The conquerors' feasts.
(exit)

CLARE:
(To find Lady Bono who is at hand)
I could not tell her
I wish to be a virgin nun.
To devote my love to purity,
My life to prayer,
And I see as a sign a mirror of
The crucified Christ.

PLENARY INDULGENCES

LADY BONO:
There is in town
A poor holy man
From a rich and powerful family from Assisi
Who has given up all his wealth
To follow his vision of God,
And lives with a few others
Rebuilding the church of San Damiano
And a rundown rectory near it.

CLARE:
What does he say
That we don't know?

LADY BONO:
They say he follows Christ alone,
Even giving all his money to the poor,
Preaching their special gifts,
And tells the idle rich
They can only go to heaven
If they abandon the good life.
"Come follow me," he pleads.
Some do and many do not.
He cures the sick, raises up the dead,
Takes the place of John the Baptizer,
And teaches the young and old
By speaking simple parables,
So all can pray together.

CLARE:
Let us quietly go,
And see who this miracle man is,
Since he is a local boy
I don't expect too much.

SCENE 2
*(In the Assisi town square, some people are watching the twitching
FRANCESCO. As he preaches his gesticulates and wildly spins around like a
top.)*

FRANCESCO:
Listen well, my friends,
Listen well, I am one of you,
Remember me as the troubadour,
The knight, the warrior who was captured

In the glorious service of Assisi.
My father sells you bolts
Of colored cloth, my mother prays
For your good causes.

OBSERVER:
It is the crazy Bernardone,
Who gave up his inheritance,
For a cloak and sandals.
His father disinherited him
In this very public square.
Only the good misguided bishop
Saved him from a well-deserved beating.
Now he and other ingrates
Beg for coins and preach the Gospel we know.
Few people have followed in awe,
This man is just a jester.

FRANCESCO:
If so, I am fool for God,
What do I ask of you
That is so horrendous,
Give up your wealth,
Pray for poverty,
Follow the Gospels,
Love God above all,
Come follow me.
When I was captured in Perugia,
I would wait, for my father I knew
Would come, and bring me home.
He is a noble man,
I respect and love him,
But we no longer heed the word of man,
We live gallantly in a new way.

CLARE:
What happened after you came home?

FRANCESCO:
I did not fit back in,
My heart changed violently,
I became addicted to the Lord,
I left my family's bounty,
I walked away from my father,
Denounced his wealth,
And began to repair

The church of Saint Damiano.
I thought that was God's will,
For He said, "Fix my church,"
And I did with lumber and cement,
Charged to my father.

But when I finished,
He appeared arguing,
"Fix my church"
"I did," I protested,
"With little help from you, my Lord."
"No, fix my Church,"
And then I realized
He meant the whole Church of Rome,

CLARE:
The whole Church of Rome!
You would have to be a pope!

FRANCESCO:
No, a pope can't do it,
Only the common people
Can bear that responsibility.
We must begin one soul at a time.

CLARE:
And is there no room for women
In your reform movement.
Can we not bear this world
Of cloaks and sandals,
Begging and praying together?

FRANCESCO:
I cannot see why not,
I cannot leave aside
Half of God's creation.
But you cannot begin in public,
There are too many perils for women,
You must stay in a convent,
And we must take care of your needs too.

CLARE:
Some of us did come
With dowries like brides
Devoted to God as virgin spouses.

FRANCESCO:
I wish it were so,
The young men want you to marry
Rather than be reformers,
To sit in your fine houses,
With your spouse and think of grandchildren,
Not isolated daughters
Praying for themselves
And unseemly beggars.

CLARE:
What vows do you take?

FRANCESCO:
The bishop will insist
That you take vows that are familiar,
Benedictine work and ethics:
To be silent, to work the full fields,
To pray six times a day
To hold a community together,
To acquire land in common.

CLARE:
And what do you say?

FRANCESCO:
I follow Jesus more closely—
The poor of spirit
The virtues of poverty, chastity, and obedience.
As for me, I value nothing,
To live in the fields that are not ours.
Even the Son of Man does not have
A foxhole to lay down his body in,
Neither will we.

CLARE:
It is a hard regime.

FRANCESCO:
If it were not so hard
I could not promise you,
A night of peace for a beautiful girl.
I fear you are too young for this life,
Too pretty to live in the world so withered,
To speak and argue with unbelievers.

CLARE:
Let me make my own decisions.

FRANCESCO:
You talk like a queen,
So do it.
Do you have others with you?

CLARE:
Perhaps by my example
Girls and older women will come.
Do they have your blessing
And that of Holy Mother church?

FRANCESCO:
I can speak only for me,
I welcome a women's order
Standing and praying side by side.
I know God will welcome it.
This is up to you, Clare.
You will get much in return.
And you have so much to lose.
Wait until you are older,
You are so young and pretty
For such an irrevocable decision.
Come back in six months.

CLARE:
That is your gospel: poverty, chastity,
Obedience, and due delay.

FRANCESCO:
I did not say that!

CLARE:
Surely, you did,
You call men to your order,
Ruffians, foreign men, so rebellious,
Some still pray to an unknown God.

FRANCESCO:
You have a harsh tone, sister.
Come in a month with your women
To the church of San Damiano,
And we will have a ritual,
Demanding and loving at that time.

(she exits)

FRANCESCO:
(Turns to his disciple Elias)
You will be assigned to work with her.
I find her too attractive
And too willful for me.

SCENE 3

CLARE:
We will support ourselves,
Until we share our bread
With the men and all our sisters.
We are all staring outward
While praying together.

(To LADY BONO)
Pray with me:
Let us recall how Francesco prays
To the large, anxious crowd.

(They repeat)
Certainly you know the great Lord
Who came out the Virgin's womb
Chose to appear contemptible,
Needy, and poor to the world.
He did that so that human beings,
Who were utterly poor and needy,
Suffering from a dire lack of heavenly food,
Might be made rich in Him,
In the kingdom of heaven
That they will certainly possess.
So exhaustingly and rejoice,
Filled with great joy and spiritual happiness.

CLARE:
Oh, great joy,
This is our goal—
An eternal joy—
That is lost beyond the vale of tears
Into a vision of the Blessed One.
I thought I would not
Like to listen to Francesco,
He was so dirty and scruffy,

But he is surrounded
By an arch of light,
For he is blessed already,
Here in front of us,
Here in our town,
Here in our short time.

LADY BONO:
He is a blessed one,
Who speaks Christ's words
In such a clear and convincing way.
I felt I understood the problems,
I felt I knew the Lord's prayers.
Better than the Apostles,
So the Scriptures are vivid and live,
I can walk with Him in Galilee.

CLARE:
Yes, yes,
I can smell the salt air of far away Galilee,
Taste the food given to the multitudes,
Hear a sound voice
Promising me the beatitudes.
Go, Lady Bono, and see
If there are others
Who wish to make a sacred visit
To the poor man of Assisi.
(exits LADY BONO)
Oh, Father am I ready for You,
For You alone to be my love?
How can I give up all
For a life of poverty,
To be sealed in a quiet convent,
Devoid of conversation and movement,
To be gone from my family,
Blind to the beautiful colors
Of the palace, surrounded by
Its blossoming flowers and its trees?
With the sameness of home
Of a convent wall,
Forbidden to speak and sworn
To chastity, poverty, and obedience.
I will never know children,
Mine or those of others.
Smilingly in loneliness,
The devil will creep in

Passing as an archangel
Assigned to give me divine advice.
(LADY BONO returns)
We have three more:
The queen's maid, Barbara,
The kitchen maid, Gertrude,
And yes, your sister Catherine!

CLARE:
No, no, not Catherine
It would be too much for Mother,
Her two daughters in one night.
Monaldo will send an army
To drag us back.

SCENE 4

(FRANCESCO is anxiously waiting at the crypt in the chilly church, with cracking Romanesque columns. He and several of his friars are marking time to see if CLARE and her companions will come after all.)

FRANCESCO:
Oh, if the holy Clare comes
And if she accepts our vows,
We enter a whole new world,
One that enrolls women of God,
Elias, you welcome her.

ELIAS:
Of course, she is a beautiful girl.

FRANCESCO:
Yes, too beautiful.
Will she give up all that admiration
To live like poor beggars?

ELIAS
Her hair is so long and blonde,
It shapes the face.

FRANCESCO:
That then is the first sacrifice,
To sheer the blonde curls
And cover her with a white veil.
Which will hide her soul
And her beauty under modesty.

(In walks CLARE, LADY BONA, and two other companions. She modestly looks at FRANCESCO)

(FRANCESCO nods)

ELIAS:
Welcome, ladies, sit here
On the stone benches.
They are cold,
But it is cold all over here.

FRANCESCO:
O blessed purity
That promises eternal life
To those who love and embrace it.
(Then he starts dancing, jittering around)
O holy poverty,
God promises the kingdom of heaven
And goes to eternal glory
And a happy, happy life
To those who possess and leave it.

(FRANCESCO' companions start chanting)
O blessed poverty!
O noble poverty!

(FRANCESCO continues and then adds to the refrain)
Noble poverty,
That the Lord Jesus Christ
Who rules and is ruling
Heaven and our only earth,
Whose Father acted in six days
And all we know was made,
So He could embrace us
Before any other creatures
And sister wind.
O, beloved poverty,
O, noble poverty.

Let me remind you:
The foxes have dens of their own,
The birds of the sky have nests
But the Son of Man,
The Christ Jesus, has no place
To lay his head, and in the end

He laid here as He gave up the ghost.

CLARE:
Oh, mystery of the cross,
Noble poverty, holy poverty
We who are from wealth,
Must give it up to the poor,
So we can be poor in spirit
To be with Christ on the cross.
I am so cold sitting,
But my brow is warm
Thinking of Christ crucified.

LADY BONO:
Holy poverty!
Noble poverty!
Take us away.

(Monks start chanting again)
Holy poverty!
Noble poverty.

A world of no violence,
No hurt, no sad children,
No husbands at war,
Or widows wrapped in death garb.
We will only know the Savior.
(Monks start up again, "Holy poverty! Noble poverty!")

CLARE:
The time has come
To devote my life
To the simple way,
To the convent,
To the pure poverty of Christ.

FRANCESCO:
Let us pray
To the virgin womb.
To a world where poverty
Is worth more than diamonds,
And reassures all heaven
That grace cannot be stolen,
But only given away to the saints.
So we must become as saints,
Poor on earth, rich in heaven.

(CLARE and her companions stand up and FRANCESCO invites them to a modest dinner and they stay)

ELIAS:
Holy Clare, if this is your way,
We have no quarters for women.
You will stay with the Benedictines
Up upon the flat hill,
And be a part of their great convent.

CLARE:
I do not wish to follow
The rule of Benedict, but of Francesco.

FRANCESCO:
I have no special women's rule,
It must be approved by the pope.
If you wish to wait,
Until we complete our restrictions…

CLARE:
No, we will go to the Benedictines,
But note well we will be back,
And observe soon the ways
Of the poor man of Assisi.

FRANCESCO:
We are just a collection
Of migrant poor men,
The Benedictines are a noble order
With a long history of service to the Church.
They are used to protecting holy young women
Like you and your companions.

CLARE:
We will go there,
But I will be back to ask to be
The first sisters of Francesco.

(They sit and eat and a strong ray surrounds them that can be seen even outside the crypt in the full town)

ELIAS:
See, it is the rainbow of ecstasy,
The light of Christ that leads the way.

He wishes all of us to live together
In poverty and obedience to the Gospels.

(They rise up and FRANCESCO begins to cut the women's hair as a tentative sign of entrance to his order. FRANCESCO cuts Clare's long gold hair which tumbles to the stone floor in a pile. She modesty prays as it falls, and FRANCESCO covers her head with a white veil. She turns to him, and gently pushes his cloak aside and takes his nipple in her mouth)

CLARE:
Now we are one.

FRANCESCO *(startled)*
Yes, we are one.

CLARE:
Yes, one in God.

FRANCESCO:
…We are one, Clare.

(Light slowly fades out)

ENTR'ACTE
(A group of town thugs seize one of FRANCESCO' monks and rip off his garb and begins to reenact the Crucifixion).

THUG 1:
Here, this a good dark spot
For the new crucifixion.

MONK:
No, no, in Christ's name.

THUG 1:
Exactly, in His name.
Set down the cross
And tie him tight.
You praise the crucified One.
Let us see how well
You can imitate him.
(They tie his hands and legs and pull up the cross between two large rocks)

THUG 2:
Good show, my Christ.

PLENARY INDULGENCES

THUG 1:
Put up the same sign:
"Jesus of Nazareth, the king of the Jews."
Write it in Latin too.

THUG 2:
There, now Lord,
Come down from the cross.
If you are the Holy One,
A follower of God the Father,
Call forth an archangel
To set you free.
Ah, no,
He misjudged—
He set free Barabbas.

THUG 1:
Curse your God,
He has forsaken you.
How stupid you are to pray
To a crucified criminal,
A wayward Jew,
Who forgot the Scriptures.

THUG 2:
Mother, behold your son,
Son, behold your mother.
The rest went home,
They ran away.

THUG 1:
No God could
Save his masterful son,
But there are no gods,
He does not exist—
Enjoy this life,
Enjoy its pleasures.
A bottle of good cheap wine is
More of an asset than a rosary.

THUG 2:
Speak, Son of Christ,
One of Francesco's poor children.

175

(A wolf appears and goes to attack the thugs. They run screaming, "The devil, the devil." Wolf walks over to the cross and eats through the rope, and the monk falls down. Wolf walks slowly away.)

MONK:
Those who killed God
Still believe in evil.
I do not grant them forgiveness
For they know what they did.
I do love
The wolf who must be a
Sincere friend of Francescoand his men.

ACT II, SCENE 1

MONALDO:
I swear to God, I cannot find her.
I have searched the plaza,
The shops, the local churches,
The estates of her friends.
I have failed my master,
I was to be the officer in charge,
My brother meant me to protect
The family's interests and its fate.
And now, the lovely Clare
Is gone, out of my sight and care.
Her mother says she does not know
Where she is—how can a mother
Not know that a girl is
Missing for a week?
What have we overlooked?
There is no mercy
For a faithless guard as me.

SOLDIER:
We have looked everywhere,
You have searched every nook
In Assisi and no trail.
She is hiding
Like a cloistered nun.

MONALDO:
A clustered nun...
That must be it.
She is in one of those cells
For widowed, married women,
Praying all day and night to God,
And sealed away from the wayward world
In endless solicitation and fasting.

(They exit).

SCENE 2

CLARE:
(Walks in and writes at desk)
My dear Catherine,

Please,
I have not left you,
But gone to find Christ
Through the steady intercession of Francesco,
The poor man of Assisi.
I now come to worship
Christ as I look in a mirror,
In gazing, determined to concentrate
On His wounds—
See his crown of bloody thorns,
The marks on his palms and feet,
The slice in his side,
Such passion for us sinners,
I feel those pains,
I can smell the filthy crowds,
Hear the jeering soldiers,
And the crucified Christ
Is looking at me, me alone
And His mother flashes back
The images of Him who saved me.
I wish to dedicate
My life to that mirror image.
(As she continues to write, her sister CATHERINE enters)
Catherine, oh no, not you.

CATHERINE:
I knew you would be here
In one of these smaller convents,
You talked often of marrying
The Lord God and not the young count.

CLARE:
The bishop has promised to protect me,
Even the vilest brigand
Will not violate his edict.
But our uncle Monaldo
Will track us down
By following you,
He is like a hunting dog.

(Loud noise and Monaldo and soldier push back the nuns and enter boisterously.)

MONALDO:
I knew it would be
Too soon for you

To be away from your sister.
I am the loyal liege
Of your father.
I command you in his name
To come home with me,
And you Clare must soon marry.

CLARE:
I am already married.

MONTALDO:
What?
Oh God, forgive me,
Your father will see
That my soul goes to hell.
Who is the miscreant?

CLARE:
It is the crucified Christ,
He made me his spouse,
Now I will live both as
A virgin and a loving bride.

MONALDO:
Nonsense,
(He grabs her veil and pulls it away.)
Oh, my God.
What has happened to your golden locks,
They added a proud dimension
To your beautiful face.
It was the real young Clare,
The real light of our lives.

CLARE:
This symbolizes to all
My marriage to Christ.
Lady Bono also wished to join
With a girl who had already
Given up her hair.
I have lived in a convent.
I am protected by the bishop.

MONALDO:
You are a living infamy
To your family and to your father.
How do I explain this?

He is off protecting the faith,
And I could not protect his daughter?
(points to CATHERINE)
Well, you are still
A girl in our family.
Come here,
(He pulls her golden hair, and she screams. He pulls her closer to him.)

Scream as you will,
But you shall come,
A second mistake in this family.
(He again pulls her hair)
(Clare starts crying; and other nuns come in, and total chaos reigns)
Listen to me, my niece,
Women are meant to serve,
To breed, to be commanded.
It is in the nature of things.
I represent your father,
But he is never home,
Doing good deeds for strangers,
Carrying the cross to heathens.
Your mother is a fine woman,
But she has taken a great estate and turned it into
A home for the poor and the wretched of the earth.
We are constantly picking up after
Her mistakes and then making them right.
The way nobles live.
She enjoys a world of romantics,
Of singers of ballads
In France, Belgium, and now Italy.
They charm women and each other,
But none puts in a day's work.
You, Catherine, will make a good marriage,
Or I will have failed once again...
And I shall not fail.
(He pulls her hair, she screams again.)
I will pull you across the plaza
As an example to women living
Below their class and status.
Women get their position
By eating the poor crumbs
Off their husband's table.

(He moves toward the door with her, and the screaming continues.)

SOLDIER:
Monaldo, enough, the plaza
Will be filled with people now,
And the old ladies will tell
All the community of your deeds,
The lord master will be more angry
If he hears of a disgraceful scene.
It reflects poorly on his knighthood,
They are sworn to peace and quiet.

MONALDO:
Then he should be here
Governing his estates,
Not leaving me with these women.

SOLDIER:
Yes, of course
But look at these women,
They are all crazy,
Who would marry them
Or want to breed with them.
They live in a convent
Because only they can permit
Each to be together.
Legend has it that they even
Menstruate at the same time.

MONALDO:
Good God, what a fate
For poor young men.
No wonder Francesco
Lives celibate and begs—
It is he and that fat bishop
Who permitted all this in Assisi.
No pope created these orders!
Let us go and see Francesco
And thrash him good,
And bring the bishop to see
The bounty of his leadership.
(exit)

CLARE:
(rushing to LADY BONO)
Go, quickly to Francesco
And to the bishop.
Tell them what you know.

Assisi needs no more chaos
And wants no more death and violence.

(exit LADY BONO)
CLARE prays quietly.

SCENE 3
(In the street MONALDO and SOLDIER hunt for FRANCESCO. And there in the center near the cathedral they find him and the bishop standing together. Behind the bishop are six knights who protect the church's interests.)

MONALDO:
Ah, there you are false saint.
You have spread your curses
On two of my young women,
I have come to exorcize your curses.

FRANCESCO:
I have no curses
But those we hear at night,
You know I have no wealth,
No land, no inheritance.
I am disenfranchised
By my own father in this very plaza.

MONALDO:
You are a demon,
Son of Satan who preaches
The gospel of hate and rejection.

FRANCESCO:
I only fast and beg,
And preach the real Gospel.

BISHOP:
Yes, that is true.

MONALDO:
And you, false bishop,
While my brother
Fights for the faith,
You let this aching worm
Seduce wealthy widows
And gay maids.
Francesco, you are in your thirties,

She is only a girl,
Get your pleasures somewhere else.
Degenerate dog, I'll beat you. *(raises a cane)*

BISHOP:
No, no violence.
Your lovely mistresses have made their decisions,
From prayer and just advice.

MONALDO:
Look at you—
Do you know poor Clare
Fasts totally three days a week,
And eats only bread and water.
How then she has become such,
Did you not notice that?

FRANCESCO:
No, I didn't notice.
I rarely see her.
I have another friar visit them
To see to their needs.

MONTALDO:
Why, her beauty is too much to ponder,
A temptation for a celibate?

BISHOP:
I did not notice,
That she was weak from fasting.

MONALDO:
And when last did
You fast, your Excellency?
You rank in weight like an Italian cardinal.
While you can enjoy food,
She insists God has her fasting
Endlessly. Even Christ loved
Food and wine; the Gospels
Tell us that He performed
His first miracle at Cana.
Give them more wine, his mother consoled,
No, did Jesus give us less wine?

BISHOP:
Easy, my boy.

MONALDO:
Our sacred Christ ate well,
He was strong and powerful,
Else how could He suffer
So much pain on Good Friday?

BISHOP:
Francesco, maybe you have to tell her
That fasting must be in moderation.

FRANCESCO:
Yes...yes.

MONALDO:
And she wears, we are told
A harsh belt so she can
Feel more pain than necessary,
Dedicated to Christ Jesus.
Tell me, bishop, let me see
The belt below your belly,
She wears terribly rough cloth,
And you Francesco
With all your penance,
Do you wear such a belt
Under that ragged tunic?
What hypocrites you are!
You told the young and the dull
That life should avoid pleasure,
You turn Christianity into an ordeal,
That is why the wise and sound
Do not pray with you
Except on Christmas and Easter.

I am not a man of severe faith,
But I ask God to curse
Your lax and hypocritical ways.
We should join with both of you.

BISHOP:
I will excommunicate you!

MONALDO:
I am ready for the battle,
You have seduced my nieces,
And deprived them of good lives,

Of the fruits of nobility,
Of children-loving husbands,
That is not Christianity,
It is a weird paganism.

BISHOP:
The knights are here
To protect me. Go home, Monaldo
And I will forgive you.

MONALDO:
You will forgive me?
Francesco, go home too,
For you are a sick, sick boy,
Once you were a gallant warrior
I respected,
Now a pathetic beggar.

(MONALDO and SOLDIER leave)

BISHOP:
You had better see what Clare
Is doing. It would be best
If she were to follow the Rule of Benedict.
He is more moderate than your rule,
Especially for women,
And from what I gather
You may have been be too harsh
For you and your own.
Cells of monks in South Italy complain.

SCENE 4

CLARE:
My sister, to reach God
You must gaze at His crucified body,
Consider well His pain,
Contemplate how His sufferings
Freed us from the sin of Adam,
And then imitate Jesus in all His glory,
But remember in our day-to-day living
We must keep faith with the way of Francesco.
See into the soul of God,
Look at a mirror
And strive for your true identity.

The Trinity itself is
A love that knits three persons together.
(enter FRANCESCO)
Oh my God, it is brother Francesco,
(They embrace and sit down.)
I did not know you were coming.

FRANCESCO:
Nor did I, but the bishop
Has implored me to speak to you.
Your family is concerned
That you are fasting yourself to death.
It is pleasant for you to raise yourself to God,
But be moderate,
For a starving girl
Cannot offer up the envy of the world.
(He then sees CATHERINE)
Happily, please let me meet your sister.
And this is your Catherine?

CLARE:
Indeed, she wishes to enter
The order you have established.

FRANCESCO:
I am going to Rome
To ask Innocent III
To approve my Rule,
He is an ambitious and powerful pope,
But he knows the house is collapsing,
And he must do something.
I offer an odd alternate life—
Jesus on the road through Galilee
If he opposes me—I can say sadly
That I am but a lowly voice in the wilderness.
Wait till I come back, sister.

CLARE:
I will if you make Catherine
As you did us an initiate
In the Franciscan way of life.

FRANCESCO:
Lady, I can only pray over you,
And cut off a bit of your hair also,
But you too must wait until

I come back from the Holy City.
(He then cuts off a few braids.)
If I am successful,
Word will be sent to create
A new convent of Clare
In Prague, and you will take
The name of Agnes,
The sweet virgin who gave up
Her life to the ancient church.
Remember, sisters, remember
That in the end God is our rule.
(he exits)

CLARE:
(takes Agnes in her arms and cries out)
O, beloved poverty
That offers us eternal glory,
And a blessed holy life
What we need is
God-centered poverty
From One who rules from the cross,
The tree of eternal life,
Poverty is the language of love.
And God lives in the logic of the cross,
Do you see that, dear Agnes?

AGNES:
I think I do,
But it is a paradox,
For we who were born to wealth.
To wish for poverty,
To assign God the unity of love
In the status which so many
Wish to leave behind.

CLARE:
You will see—
Now let us pray,
That Francesco will see the pope,
And we all are made legitimate.

SCENE 5

(Light focusing on Pope Innocent III in full regalia, and before him is a kneeling FRANCESCO and his companions. The pope seems hesitant, but blesses them, and they leave. He reaches into his vestments and gives FRANCESCO a silver rosary and his worn Bible).

SCENE 6

CLARE:
(excited)
Tell Agnes—
Agnes, Francesco had gotten
High approval from the pope.
We have a rule we can all use,
But the bishops are reluctant
That women in the order
Stand out and beg for alms
For it will lead to abuses
From licentious men.
So the friars will beg for us too.

AGNES:
They will not like that.

CLARE:
No, I am afraid they will not.
To support themselves is hard enough.
Now Agnes, you will leave
For a convent in Trent
And then prepare to go to Prague.
Oh, we will miss
Each other and pray together.
I will offer up my communions
For your missionary work.

(AGNES vanishes)
Now, poverty is more than earthly riches,
You have chosen between the things of heaven
And the stolen goods of the earth.
You will reap a fine crown
And earn eternal life.
Love is the Father, Son and Holy Spirit.
Enter deeply into God's mystery,
Embrace the true meaning of life.

SCENE 7
(Two Franciscan friars are walking and conversing)

FRANCISCAN 1:
He has pushed too hard.

FRANCISCAN 2:
Him and us too.

FRANCISCAN 1:
He rarely eats,
Prays all night,
Never sleeps in the day,
Enjoys few of God's benefits
Made for the body.
I know that this is our way.
Poverty, austerity, chastity,
But that has left his frame weak,
He looks close to death,
His venture to Morocco
To convert the Arabs
Let his eyes go blind
From the blazing sand.
In the end the sheiks admired him,
But he cannot even blame
The problems on us or on himself.
Is that a way to serve God?
We should use our eyes to see
God's works, our noses to smell
The fragrant flowers,
The touch of soft silk,
Not these rough clothes.

FRANCISCAN 2:
This is our way,
We knew it when we came,
It was our attraction
To be poorer than the poor,
More vagabond than homeless,
The way was the way of Christ Jesus.
Were we wrong?
He said sell all we had
And give it away,
We did that and now
We live in huts like animals.
And the greatest of men
Lives close to death
In that thatched mud hut,
Unable to swallow,
Unable to see the host of Christ.
He tried so hard to be Jesus
To lay down in the earth

And call it home.
Not to have a family—
He is lonely with his God,
And his questions are not answered.

FRANCISCAN 2:
May God bless this good man.
We have called Clare to come.
She is his only true friend,
Who understands what he is doing
With his life and ours.

FRANCISCAN 1:
She will not come,
She is a hermit.
Rules her convent with a gentle hand,
But never leaves.
In many ways
She is stricter than he is.

FRANCISCAN 2:
He will wait until she comes
Before he dies,
To touch her hands,
Since he is wedded to her beauty.

FRANCISCAN 1:
The bishop has said
They will build an elegant chapel
To honor his bones,
And let Christians know
That the last Christian did not die
On the cross on Calvary.

FRANCISCAN 2:
The last monument Francesco would want
Is a fine temple,
He would be buried under a tree,
Where the breezes can cut across
His grave site, and he can be frozen
In a wooden box,
And who will remember
The poor man of Assisi?

(Enter CLARE:)

FRANCISCAN 1:
Ah, we knew you would come,
He cannot live
Without saying farewell
To you, dear Clare.

CLARE:
(upset)
Oh, where is he?
Is it as bad as your monks
Say to my nuns?
Is he near the end?

FRANCISCAN 2:
He is very sick,
And he has asked to be stripped
Naked, so he can decompose faster.

CLARE:
Oh, beloved brothers,
Let me go to the hut,
You need to hurry.

(She runs off to the hut)

FRANCISCAN 1:
She is still beautiful
And so stately.
How she decided to take the walk,
To bear the burdens
To toss away all she once had.
Beauty should last forever,
As spring should never turn to winter.

FRANCISCAN 2:
And when this is all said and done
Who will remember Clare?
For women are even more
Forgotten than the poorest men.
(exit)

SCENE 8
(The death of CLARE, 17 years later after FRANCESCO. She had become a hermit in her convent since 1236, the death of FRANCESCO. POPE

INNOCENT IV comes in to visit CLARE's body. He has with him a long line of acolytes and bishops.)

INNOCENT IV:
We have promised her our approval and our vow,
And she died with our scroll in her hand,
What a smile that beautiful face had,
What an elegant young woman she must have been,
For even the old lady
Is striking, still wearing a mask of beauty.
(Turns to the BISHOP)
First, Francesco and then her.
You know Clare is also a saint,
A true follower of Francesco
And of the immortal Christ.
We wish now to declare her a saint,
Is it not obvious—
Let us do it by a voice choice,
Let the people be inspired.

BISHOP:
No, no you cannot.
You will violate our own canon laws.
If she, then who else
Will we make a saint quickly,
It will cheapen sainthood in the public eye.

INNOCENT IV:
(Angrily takes the canon law book and throws it at the bishop's chest.)
Here, you have one full year
To find the reasons for her sainthood,
No more, no less.
For we all know we were in
The presence of a saint in life
Why not acknowledge it in death?

BISHOP:
People will forget her,
Who remembers a woman anyhow?
She is no Francesco.

INNOCENT IV:
We will remember her,
And if we are correct in heaven
She sits with God at His right hand,
Near the Blessed Virgin—

Another woman in heaven,
Closer to Jesus than any man
Before or since,
A woman full of heroic virtue,
Who taught us how to love.
Oremus, Santa Clara.

(In the background is the song of Saint Francis:)

"Lord, make me an instrument of your peace.
Where there is hatred, let me bring love.
Where there is discord, let me bring union.
Where there is error, let me bring truth.
Where there is doubt, let me bring faith.
Where there's despair, let me bring hope.
Where there is darkness, let me bring your light.
Where there's sadness, let me bring joy.
O Master, let me not seek as much
To be consoled as to console,
To be understood as to understand,
To be loved as to love.
For it is in giving that one receives,
It is in self-forgetting that one finds.
It is in pardoning that one is pardoned,
In giving of ourselves that we receive,
It is in dying that one is raised to eternal life."

BISHOP:
What a troubadour.

INNOCENT IV:
What a lady.

DIVINE MERCY IN MY SOUL:

A PLAY ON THE LIFE OF ST. FAUSTINA KOWALSKA

Dedicated to Maureen Digan
the first certified miracle for
the canonization of Sister Faustina,
the Apostle of Divine Mercy,
and to her devoted husband, Robert.

DIVINE MERCY IN MY SOUL:
A PLAY ON THE LIFE OF ST. FAUSTINA KOWALSKA

ACT I

Recitation: "Godsinki" or "Little Hours of the Immaculate Conception"

Zacznijcie wargi nasze, chwalić Pannę świętą,
Zacznijcie opowiadać cześć jej niepojętą.
Przybądź nam miłościwa pani, ku pomocy,
A wyrwij nas z potężnych nieprzyjaciół mocy.
Chwała Ojcu, Synowi Jego Przedwiecznemu,
I równemu Im w Bóstwie Duchowi Świętemu.
Jak była na początku i zawsze i ninie,
Niech Bóg w Trójcy Jedyny na wiek wieków słynie

(On stage, walks a young nun dressed in a simple black habit)

Good Lord, when I was a mere seven years old,
I felt a calling, a vocation
From God, but I did not know
What the silver light that bathed me was.
And no one else knew what it was.
I first met God at St. Casimir Church.
People said, "You dreamt it,
So forget it, girl," and I did.
We were a poor, ragged family in Lodz,
I worked the farm.
And I was also a housemaid in town.
We had thirteen acres,
And the soil was so barren.
We loved God and Mary as a family does,
Said our prayers and sang the songs
To which all of Poland knelt down.

One evening, my sister and I ventured out
And went to a dance at the park.

I can still hear the enchanting polkas,
Feel the vibrations,
And remember how wonderful
It was to dance,
To twirl my dress, to love life.
I was happy that night
And pleased to be with
So many young people.
But then, I alone heard
The voice of Jesus.

Why do you ignore Me?

I was in a state of shock.
I sat in the corner by myself
On a folding chair.
Then quietly I left the dance,
Went to a nearby church—
For in those days the churches
Were always open and full.

I fell down on my knees,
Got my new dress dirty,
And I lay flat on my face,
Praying for God and His clear, dear guidance.
He told me to become a nun,
To not neglect Him, as so much
Of the world in all its forms does.
But—no, I cannot go—
Why my mama, my daddy—
They have already commanded
I cannot leave and be a nun.
I will marry and have their grandchildren,
That is what they want from me.
I am too pretty to be in a cloister,
They say.
But what of Jesus' command?
"He doesn't come to girls so young,
Who are barely women.
No, no."

Why do you neglect Me so?

Jesus, I cannot disobey,
They love me.

I love you more and
My family lasts for all eternity.
Go to Warsaw and offer yourself up
To be a nun.

And so I obeyed Jesus,
My new spouse and my Redeemer.
I saw Jesus all covered with wounds,
Whipped and crucified,
A victim of my sins.
I took the carriage to the station
And then a train to Warsaw.
I did not tell my parents of my leaving,
I gazed out of the dirty window panes
Of the sturdy wooden train,
And I cried, and cried, and cried.
And then I feel asleep as the train
Swayed and grew warmer.
Gone were my family, my friends, my life.
Was I dealing with Jesus,
Or with an illusion in my own mind?

When I arrived in my one dress
I went from one convent to another
Until I found
The Sisters of Our Lady of Mercy
On Zytima Street.
I went to the large dark door,
And knocked, and then
A tall abrupt sister opened up
The portal only a crack.
"I wish to enter your convent,"
I said, and she let me in.
We talked as we stood in the foyer,
I never even made it inside—
"You are rather young,
You are rather uneducated,
You have no skills,
You are not fit for
Our evangelical efforts for girls in trouble.
And what—
You are poor and have no money.
You cannot be a bride of Christ
Without a dowry.
Brides come to their lovers,
Especially the Lord, with dowries.

We cannot support a poor girl here.
She later wrote her superiors, I am told—
"Helen is not a particularly
Significant person."

And so I left, roamed the city,
Became a cook and a nanny,
Teaching children the lives of the saints,
Lives I also loved to recount.
I wished from then on to become a saint.
But I feared if I could not—
I would go into the purifying fires
Of a long, deep purgatory,
Sealed off from God and his beloved Son.

I saved money as best I could, sixty zlots,
And applied to the convent again,
And God be praised,
I was let in.

To all the Sisters of Our Lady, thank God.
They called me Sister Faustina,
And I added "of the Blessed Sacrament."
I was no longer Helen,
But I was divided from my family,
A girl with no friends.

Like all young nuns,
I prayed for guidance—
What should I do to satisfy God—
Where is He?
Why must He hide from me?
What do I do now?
I soon came to dislike the convent.
Maybe it was homesickness,
But I wanted to pray more,
Not peel potatoes,
Answer the door,
Or clean the floors near the chapel.
I needed a new order—
One with more contemplation,
One with more time to pray.
Else how will I get to know God
And earn salvation?
Can I help the souls in purgatory—
Are those in hell

PLENARY INDULGENCES

Too far gone even for God's mercy?

Then early on, oh, so very early,
Jesus appeared to me—

> **Pray for the souls in purgatory.**
> **For those souls cannot pray for themselves.**
> **They must just burn and repent.**

In a flash, the vision darkened
And I was walking unsteadily
Through the circle of purgatory.
Those poor people were writhing,
Crying, moaning, and asking for mercy.
"Mercy, only mercy,
For none of us wants from God
Justice, that is too terrible,
But mercy, only mercy."

My angel guided me to them—
"Pray for us, for we cannot help ourselves,
Gain us mercy so we can see God.
Our pain is blindness to His Glory.
We long for him,
Only Mary gives us some refreshment.
But when she leaves,
We are still alone.
Oh, Mother of God, help us."

My head swirled,
The angel caught my step.
What shall we do?
And then I heard:

> **My mercy does not want this.**
> **Justice demands it.**
> **Pray for them—**
> **They are your special charge.**

The angel like a good mother
Led me down the side of the pit.
I was slipping suddenly away.
It would be so easy to fall into it,
And nearly impossible to get out.
I prayed for all the souls,
All I had met, all I had seen,

All I had heard, and those far beyond,
Who were in those acres of agony.

And then I stood alone again
In the convent chapel,
Under the Stations of the Cross,
Looking at the woman
Wiping away His fallen blood.
Sweet, dear Veronica.
I now knew what my mission was.

Soon I was let into the novitiate—
Two years of final preparation—
All was good for me,
But then it came like...

As I went deep into myself,
I found great misery not happiness.
Yes, I saw the holiness of God,
But I could not reach Him.
I was mere dust in the world,
Insignificant, without meaning,
And I dared not approach Him,
Even in prayer, even in the Eucharist.

The convent laid out times
For prayer, for recreation, for meals, for work.
And I often failed in obedience.
I talked too often and joked a bit.
Then in the spring of 1927,
A terrible shadow overwhelmed my soul.
I felt no joy or consolation
In simple and deep prayer.
I tried so often to meditate on God
And on His good works,
But I felt nothing but misery.

The darkness went on and on.
I could not get from the Lord a reply.
He was stubbornly silent—
But You made me come here,
To leave my family and my life.
Now You ignore me?
I knew despair and a complete darkness.
Deadly fear seized me,
And I became weak.

I came to hate all that was holy and divine,
I knew blasphemy and fear,
And emptiness and the dryness of a dark tunnel.
I could not leave, I could not escape,
I am giving, giving,
Jesus where are you?
He spoke to me but not with words of comfort.

And then six months of agony,
Passed quietly on.
I returned to my convent duties,
But now my companion sisters
Called me a slacker, a hysteric,
A woman possessed,
One who wanted special privileges.
An older nun said to me,
"God only honors saints,
You are not one, my dear."

Oh, Jesus are you an illusion after all?
And His response was:

My love deceives no one.

During this terrible time,
It grew so cold,
My feet ached with frost.
Poland is so frigid in the winter,
My soul is so cold without You.

They transferred me from one convent to another.
I never could make friends,
I never had a confessor who understood.
I needed to share the visions I had.
To talk of the despair and the fears,
To tell people I was not delusional.
I was not possessed, I was not
Trying to get out of my duties.
I turned back to Jesus,
And You did not answer.
I have nothing.
I feel sick in my stomach,
Wounded in my head,
My hands and feet seem to have painful spots,
But I do not see anything.

My God, is it like St. Francesco?

One night I was assigned to the door.
It was dark and cool outside.
The convent was surrounded by a high wall,
With an iron gate that opened at the base
To let in the poor and the devout,
Who would come from the town and the farms.
Poland after the war was a hungry place,
That lived on little,
And prayed well.

That gloomy and cold night,
I saw a ragged man coming in.
I was afraid to open the door at first,
But he wanted food.
And so I gave him a bowl of soup and bread—
That was all we had for dinner—
He gratefully took it and walked down the hill,
Down to the open gate.
He turned and looked at me—
Oh, that was the face of Jesus—
Just as I had seen it,
And then He vanished into the night,
The eternal night before me.
What was He saying?
What was He doing?
Why my night at the door?
Later, I could see the gate
From my little cell
Through the trees down by the wall.
The gate was my soul,
My soul opened and vulnerable,
To the dark, cold nights.

Again I was transferred,
Again I became sick in my lungs.
In comparison with you, Jesus
Everything is nothing.
Sufferings are splinters
That keep my heart aflame.
You, Oh Jesus, are my reward,
The treasure of my heart.

Then I saw Him—
Oh, so clear, He was clad in white,

And looked so glorious and loving.

I had prayed so hard,
That I was weary and downtrodden.
I was not sure if it were Jesus,
Or just my mind playing with me.
Could it be Satan himself,
Disguised so as to make me vulnerable
To his evil ways.
Instead of helping people climbing
Out of the pit of purgatory.
I would be confined to it,
Or even worse to eternal hell,
Because I had followed the Evil One.

Can you not know
Me from temptation,

I heard.

I must be guided to Him.
Yes, yes, I will, pray
To the Virgin Mother.
Hail Mary, full of grace
The Lord is with thee—

My son wishes punishment for no one.
He wishes all to assume His mercy.

Blessed are thou among women,
And blessed is the fruit
Of thy womb, Jesus.

Oh, Jesus you are my only reward,
Everything is nothing.
I will suffer and be consumed
Like dry wood in the fire.

He was so sparkling, so luminous
That I lost my very breath,
My heart pounded and my palms were wet.
One hand of His was raised,
As if to give a blessing
The other touched His breast.
Two rays came from that breast—
Red and pale.

I could not stop and look,
I could not speak or move.
I was shaking in my soul.
And He seemed to know it.
Finally,

> **Paint this image of Me, with**
> **The signature, "Trust Jesus, I trust in you."**
> **I wish all to see Me**
> **Like this, so more will come to Me.**
> **This is your duty now.**
> **Do it for all the living.**
> **And those to be born.**

But I did not understand.
How could I do it?
I am an ignorant farm girl,
Not an artist.

> **I desire that this image**
> **Be mounted in your chapel.**
> **And throughout the world.**
> **I pronounce victory over all enemies**
> **On earth, and especially at the hour of death.**
> **I will Myself defend you**
> **As My own Glory.**

But I do not understand
I have questions.
Soon He vanished as He came;
His image once so bright and appealing,
Melted into the darkness
Of our harsh convent walls.

I dropped to my knees and prayed,
And I cried.
God, am I really a hysteric as they say?
A young girl whose emotions
Are running away from her.
But I did see him,
I did hear Him as clearly as our bell,
Chiming us to chapel.
So I prayed and went back to my cell.
Am I delusional, as they say?
Oh, Jesus, I trust in you—
"Jezu, Ufam Tobie."

But now how do I do your will?

It was so cold that night,
I could not sleep,
So I went and leaned near the ovens,
Stoked the hearth
To bake bread that morning.

I feared I might forget
The picture image, the pattern of Him.
But I did not—it was burned bright into my soul.
Besides, I was told—"Sister, Jesus
Was only speaking symbolically,
He wants His image in your soul.
Not a common portrait
Upon a canvas."
But as I walked in the convent,
Jesus called out firmly:

> **My image is in your soul already.**
> **I want this picture**
> **Which will be placed up in the**
> **First Sunday after Easter.**
> **That will be the Feast of Divine Mercy.**
> **Priests must proclaim it**
> **Throughout the world.**
> **Teach people to approach Me.**
> **Do not be afraid.**
> **The distrust is tearing Me apart.**
> **The distrust of a soul**
> **Causes Me even more pain.**

And then He left me to my own devices.

I went quickly to Mother Superior for guidance,
She told me to ask for a sign
That He was really revealing His will
The way I thought.

But Jesus immediately talked to me alone:

> **I will make this entirely clear to**
> **The Mother Superior in My way.**

I did not know what to do.
But the Lord had said

On judgment day, I will be
Held accountable for
A great number of souls.
I will not neglect them.
Meanwhile, the rumors started again—
"Faustina says she saw Jesus,
Can you imagine that?"
They would spy on me,
Looking even in my cell at night.
"So you are a fantasist, Sister,
You have visions…or so you say."
I talked to Mother Jane one day,
"You queer, hysterical visionary.
Get out of my room, get out!,"
She screamed.
Jesus, Jesus I cannot go on
Any longer, spare me these sufferings,
I am alone and very afraid.

Do not fear, I am with you.
You will suffer, but not without Me.

Still, I heard the whispers behind my back,
They called me "the princess,"
Me a poor farm girl,
Me Helen Kowalska.
I bitterly responded one day,
"You, are right, I am a princess
For the royal blood of Jesus
Flows in me!"

I started to sketch in charcoal,
Then I began the painting.
I was terrible at it—
And I feared that my poor efforts
Would brand me as unfit
To take my final vows.
One sister came up to me,
Unannounced and uncalled for,
To say she would do all
She could to keep me out of the order.
I shook with fear and despondency.
"Sister, you are an eccentric."
Finally I was allowed to take my final vows,
She did not prevail,
And I cried with deep joy—

"See, she is a hysteric,
She is lazy, making believe to be ill."

But I was indeed ill—
I saw clearly my true fate,
I was to be a "victim soul,"
A person who would be as Jesus was,
Able and willing to take on terrible sufferings
For the redemption of others.
Only the closest of friends
Can bring the atonement of others.

Come, join with Me.
Trust in Me.
Do My will now.
You are a delight in My eyes.
You are the delight of My heart.
I will carry you into Myself.
So you will lose yourself.
I will make you one with Me.
You will know Me
As far as has ever been done.
For God and you are not two,
Seeking to know each other.
I will envelop you
Into Myself, into
My heart, and you will be
An apostle of My mercy,
For all mankind forever.

Every day I walked by
The bare convent wall in Plock,
And it was a silent reproach.
I had not been painting,
Only doing bad sketches.
The image in my soul
Could not make it into my hand.
I worked on the portrait,
But one day
As I was sketching
I was approached
By a troubled girl.
I made a deal with God—
How arrogant of me—
If you are truly my God,
Make this girl go to confession,

That is my sign, and so it was done.

Do you believe in Me now?

I was filled with such joy,
But still other times,
Often waves of doubt
Washed over my soul.
I was glad to leave Plock
And go to Warsaw, for the sisters
Seemed to like me more there.
I spoke to no one about my visions
And never about the Divine Mercy mission.
But at a retreat,
I felt infused with the Trinity.
Oh, three-person God reveal yourself to me.

Speak to the priests
About my inconceivable Mercy.

But still I was reluctant.
I knew my world though would be
One of deep suffering.
I was to be a victim soul
Who embraces fear and loathing,
Once during Lent I re-lived
The sufferings of another nearby,
And felt the awful moments
Of deeply suicidal thoughts.
I prayed for this person,
And the thoughts left us both.

Then one day while I was trying
To better understand my mission,
My very own sister, Wanda, came to visit.
She was our youngest, and I had left
When she was an infant.
She was a guest of our community,
Visiting me, but she too
Was deeply sorrowful and depressed.
For two weeks we prayed,
And the shadows lifted.
God is good.

When she left
I went on again to Krakow,

And to my final vows.
We all laid that day
On the altar floor,
Covered by a black pall—
Dead to the world and its ways—
Each wearing a ring from our spouse, Jesus.

I was now a nun, and was assigned
To still to another place, Vilnius,
On the way, I visited the Black Madonna
At Jasna Gora and walked up
The beautiful bedazzled side aisle,
Leading up to the picture—

(Picture of Our Lady of Czestochowa lights up)

Oh, to have that portrait artist
Working for me.
To bring out in rich colors
The Divine Mercy image
As he had done for the Madonna.
All around me were kneeling people,
Whispering quiet prayers,
The people of Poland loved this portrait.
Jesus was right—
A picture is so vivid.
It is a gospel unto itself.

And then I moved once again on to Vilnius,
A small convent with a few huts
In the most isolated of places.
I missed Krakow and Warsaw,
For the world woos us in
Strange and subtle ways.
I was the chief gardener—
Meant to hoe, dig, and carry water.
I was the apostle of vegetables.
Often when I weeded I went
With a rosary in the one hand.

Then I met Reverend Michael Sopocka—
He would be the confessor I needed.
But at first, he did not believe me.
"Does she have difficulties with reality?,"
He asked my superiors.
He had a psychiatrist examine me—

And she pronounced me healthy.
Then he believed, I guess.
He gave me the name of a painter
He knew, and I was to visit
Eugene Kazimierowski, a professor,
Who lived near the convent.
I went with Mother Irene,
And we kept the visits a secret.
I directed his drawings.
I prayed and asked Jesus
What the two rays from His hands meant.

> **The pale ray is water**
> **Which makes souls righteous.**
> **The red ray is the blood**
> **Which is the life of the soul.**
> **This is the depth of My tender Mercy,**
> **When My agonized heart**
> **Was opened by a lance on the Cross.**

Father Sopocko said they were
The white of baptism,
The red of the Eucharist.
He came better
To know the secrets
Of Divine Mercy
And the secrets of my heart.
"I am in the company of a saintly nun,
Of one blessed by God," he said to Mother Irene.

Then to deal better with my feelings
And my witness, he asked me to write in a diary
All I experienced and knew.
I thought at first
He was just tired of hearing me talk,
Of my going on and on.

It started out small,
A notebook with JMJ.
Jesus, Mary and Joseph.
On top of every page.
These are the encounters
Of my soul with God.
Of His special visitations
I have so little education,
Lord, so little learning.

I am not Augustine or Ignatius.
They will laugh at me
Only the good father must see this.
It is a personal statement,
Not for others, promise?

Saturday, every Saturday,
We traveled to see the artist.
I tried to describe in words
The vividness I had seen,
How my soul was melded to Him,
How bright He was,
But how the darkness did not touch Him
As He emerged through its veil
Like a light through the fog.
His gaze was so sure and straight,
Transfixing me in my steps,
The red is blood,
The white is water—
It is the sacrifice of the Mass,
Said for all the world
By the first priest.

Paint the portrait,
Please paint it soon.
And he worked on it.

(She points to audience)

It is completed.

*(An audience member brings a covered portrait up to stage,
Places it behind her.)*

Oh, my Lord it is done!

(She quickly pulls off cover)

This can't be—
I have failed You once again.
This is not what I have seen—
It does not do justice
To Jesus, it is not Him.
I saw Him so clearly,
But this is too common,
This is too like a person—you or me—

You do not understand,
I cannot move from my heart
To his hand.
He is so grand, so bright,
And I have left Him
A collection of colors,
Of darks and lights—
But that is not my Jesus,
Oh, I have failed again.

> **Enough, my daughter, that portrait**
> **Is fine as it is.**
> **Men can describe Me**
> **In only earthly terms.**
> **Take this image,**
> **And put it into your chapel.**
> **Leave it as it is.**
> **Let it be.**
> **It is enough**
> **To suit My purposes.**
> **Let the people see Me.**
> **Bring the people to Me.**

We would sing in the convent
Hymns, ancient hymns,
To celebrate the Divine Presence:

(She sings:)

> Holy God, we praise Thy Name;
> Lord of all, we bow before Thee!
> All on earth Thy scepter claim,
> All in heaven above adore Thee.
> Infinite Thy vast domain,
> Everlasting is Thy reign.
>
> Hark! The loud celestial hymn
> Angel choirs above are raising,
> Cherubim and seraphim,
> In unceasing chorus praising,
> Fill the heavens with sweet accord.
> Holy, holy, holy Lord.

(Faustina kneels by portrait,
And the light fades out.
End of Act I) .

214

ACT TWO

FAUSTINA:
Eternal Father, I offer You
The Body and Blood, Soul and Divinity of Your
Dearly beloved Son, Our Lord Jesus Christ,
In atonement for our sins
And those of the whole world.

For the sake of His sorrowful passion
Have mercy on us and on the whole world.

For the sake of His sorrowful passion....

Those are the prayers He commissioned.
We can say them on the beads of a rosary.

> **Whoever will recite these prayers**
> **Will receive great mercy at the hour of death.**
> **Even the most hardened sinner**
> **Will receive my grace from My infinite mercy.**
> **Say this in the presence of the dying,**
> **And I will stand between My Father**
> **And the dying person, not as the just Judge**
> **But as the merciful Savior.**

Then, He gave me an even more difficult charge:
Jesus told me to found a special order
Devoted to His Divine Mercy,
A new group of devoted followers,
But I could not create a new order,
And be a member of this one.
They surely will not follow me,
I was a lesser member of these Sisters,
A quiet woman not respected by all.
"She is not a particularly significant person."
Without Jesus, I am not,
But with Him I am the Apostle of Mercy.
All of us are insignificant,
But it is said we are
Made in the very image of God.
That must mean something, doesn't it?
Oh, Blessed Virgin what should one do?

> You are significant,
> For you are my child,

And I pray for your mission.
Do as He wills, as He says.
I am going to prepare
A special place in heaven for you.

How can I be a saint?
I am so much a failure.

You are the special saint
Of His divine mercy.
People will know your name
Far beyond these walls.
The proud and the humble
Will pray to you.
"Listen to what she says,
Read what she has written,
Love this young woman,
As I do."

Sometimes I say the special prayers
Of Divine Mercy on your rosary.
And I change your requests
Given to the children at Fatima.

My rosary is meant to bring
All to my Son,
You are doing that too, my child.

And so I talked to the Blessed Virgin,
About her Son and about me.
I felt good about my sufferings,
Sure of my mission in this life.
I continued to write in my diary,
All of this and much more.
Then one week, my confessor went away
To travel to Palestine.
That very night I was visited in my dreams
By a handsome young man,
Well dressed and passionately intent.
He asked me why I kept a diary,
It was an arrogance in the eyes of God.
I should throw it into the flames,
And so I did.
All those little notebooks
With JMJ on each page
Burnt and crackled in the stove.

I must honor obedience,
I must learn to do what I am told.
There was much in there
About my early years,
My coming to Jesus and to the convent life.
It told the story of my soul
And my visions of Jesus.

When my confessor came back,
I told him of my dream,
Of my actions, and he was angry.
Did I not see, he said, that I was
Being visited not by an angel of God,
But by a demon who wished
To stop my message of Divine Mercy?
I grew frightened, then I became
Resentful that I could be so foolish,
I was like the foolish virgin
In the New Testament.
I was an ignorant farm girl
Who was taken advantage of.
I did not know what to do,
For what is destroyed
Is gone forever.
My confessor demanded that I
Recreate what I had written and
Then destroyed.
Try to remember.
I did exactly that,
But I surely did not recall all
Of what I had written,
Especially on my early years
And my first encounters with Jesus
At prayer and at St. Casimir.
Now I knew that Satan had
Decided to focus on me
For his evil works.
But why, I am so insignificant.

I tried only to be obedient to God.
Then one night as I was leaving the kitchen
Going to my cell in the convent,
I stepped out into the yard,
Not too far from where I first saw
Jesus dressed in rags that night,
Near the gate on the bottom of the hill,

And as I walked I was surrounded
By rabid dogs, black shadows,
Who circled me for an attack.
They were ready to rip me apart.
I looked at them and quietly
Prayed to Jesus for protection.
They angrily exclaimed,
"She has done it again,
She has called down Him on us.
Begone, she has cursed us
Without knowing it."
And then they were gone, all gone.
I was alone with only the breeze
As a witness to what had happened.
I had wanted so to be a saint,
But never realized that Satan
Is so powerful an enemy.
I thought I had only to fear my own
Weaknesses, my own failings,
But I was wrong.
Those stirrings were small
In comparison to Satan and his wiles.
Only God can conquer his evil angels.
May St. Michael watch over me,
Defeat the legions of black shadows,
Of the vicious, the self-righteous,
The rabid, the melancholy, the desparate.
Jesus, I trust in you.
Oh, Lord, my days of work,
Of strength and suffering have begun.
I have painted the portrait You wished,
And I have kept the diary.
Father Sopocko hung the picture in the convent
Near the church in Vilnius
Where he was pastor.
I accept Jesus's commission
And I feel all the sufferings,
The fear and terror which fill sinners.
To them I give consolations
From God Himself.
I am a mere conduit of His mercy.
I can hear their blasphemies and curses,
And it makes me feel so weary,
So full of despair for them.
And so it continued.

Then one day, my guardian angel
Demanded, "Pray for the dying."
So I gathered some girls around me
And said the rosary aloud as we weeded.
Then I heard the voice of a sister
Living not with us but in Warsaw.
"Pray for me—pray until
I tell you to stop. I am dying."

Later I heard she died in peace.
I have never before prayed
Directly for one person.

> **The prayers of a humble and loving soul**
> **Disarm the anger of My father**
> **And draw down an ocean of blessings.**

Death is indeed dreadful,
But one must realize that
The Lord's mercy is great,
And we need it at the critical hour.
I have seen many close to death.
I too know the pain.
I grow sick, grasping for breath,
My limbs become numb and I
See only darkness before me.
Sometimes I could not confess,
Or even receive the Sacrament,
In the midst of what I thought
Was the end of my life.

One gloomy night I lay in bed.
I awoke to see black figures
Swarming like bats all round my room.
They hated the poor sight of me—
"Be damned, you and He
Who is within you.
You torment us even in hell!"
But then they melted away,
Like the mists in the early morning.

I began to become stronger
And to receive the Eucharist.
I went back to my gardens,
The flowers looked so beautiful,
So vivid, so open to the sun.

They seemed to reach up
To learn to pray.

Then one day I walked from the gardens
To the chapel
And there He was again,
Jesus of Divine Mercy.
His rays of red and white flooded
The convent garden and the city beyond the gates.
Not only I, but one of the girls,
Imelda, saw strange light rays,
But not the image.

I prayed to Jesus
That the pope would declare a Sunday
To the Feast of Divine Mercy,
That would be one step
In a long walk to bring the message
To the whole needy world.
But Pius XI did not.
And I continued on,
Praying for the souls
And keeping alive His message.
I saw Jesus also as a little child too,
So I would be a child
In God's arms pleading
For hope and love.

My diary became even more of an
Intense spiritual journal to heaven.
Your will, not mine
Prevail, oh God.

I had given up my old life,
My friends and my family
To come to the convent.
Then from my superiors, I learned
That my beloved mother was dying.
I prayed for her recovery,
And she did cheat death that night.
After ten years, I was home again,
And able to spend it with my family,
Getting to know them again
To listen together to their stories,
To pray together for our souls.
We sang and played,

And then I had to leave,
To go back to the convent.
There I prayed to the Virgin Mother
And asked her if my mother and father
Would go to heaven,
And she said yes.
Then I asked her about
My brothers and sisters,
And she paused,
And I knew I had to pray
Even more intently for my brother.
Oh Lord, how can I free souls in purgatory
And not be able to see my own
In the richness of heaven?

While there I was approached
By a lady with a very sick child
Covered with puss and infection
In her eyes.
I recoiled at first from the sight,
And then I took the child in hand,
And kissed her eyes and prayed.
May God forgive my first hesitations.

During Lent at the convent,
I meditated on the Passion,
I could see Jesus being beaten,
Being cursed at, and being crucified.
Why—why was it necessary for God
To even give up one drop of blood in pain
For all the sins of man?
We are redeemed not just by His suffering,
But by His very presence on earth
How much more does He love us,
How much more does He love the Father?
Still it is so terrible,
So merciless, so horrid.
I wish I could end it,
Could substitute myself for Him.

I think over and over about those images,
I got so irritated, so weary
That I feel my mind is leaving my body.
Sometimes I need to go out
In the cold air and shock myself.
Once I saw Him strapped on a wooden beam,

Being taunted and slapped.
I felt so much hurt for Him
And I loved Him even more.
How do You do it,
How do you fight the forces of evil?

Satan and his demons are never quiet.
More and more the devils
Appeared to me as terrible beasts,
He would smash flower pots at me,
Shake my bed in the gruesome night,
Turn into a black cat
And jump at my feet.
I could not free myself,
So I prayed the rosary,
And the devils vanished.

One Good Friday, Jesus crucified
Appeared and declared:

**I desire that the image
Be publicly honored.**

Then I saw the Divine Mercy image emerge
From His dying body.
I insisted to Father Sopocko
That the image be brought out of the convent,
And be placed on the church of the Dawn Gate.

He opposed the idea,
Said there were events
Planned already there.
The day I wanted was April 28,
The Sunday after Easter.

Some complained, but the image was put there.
Thousands saw the portrait,
And no one knew of my role in this.
I left the church quietly.
And once again they appeared.
The demons moved into the streets,
Screaming "Stop tormenting us."
My guardian angel protected me from them,
He walked me back to the convent door,
Like a gentlemanly chaperone.
And once again, they became

A dark and ugly shadow.

Soon after I saw the Trinity,
A crystal with three doors.
There Jesus was saying,

**The Feast comes from
The very depths of My mercy.**

He wanted all to see and know
His Divine Mercy,
And I was the inadequate messenger.
I must show more people the image.
Finally the priests restored the picture
To the old convent,
But many people had seen it,
And it would be back in sight.
I was happy at the viewings,
But I grew frightened again.
I did not speak with Jesus
At this difficult time,
But just recited prayers.
And then one day, He would
Have no more of that neglect.

**You will prepare the world
For My final coming.**

I only desired to avoid this charge.
I left the convent in the midst of prayer.

**You cannot get away from Me.
I am everywhere.
You cannot do anything by yourself,
With Me all is possible.**

My confessor listened to my story—
And told me to follow the stirrings
Of my soul.
I apologized to Jesus,
But His forgiveness is so great

**You are my dwelling place,
Because of you, I will withhold judgment,
For your sake I will bless the world.**

I came to see more,
The fullness of the souls
And of me, of their fear,
Of their desperations.
Oh, Jesus I trust in You.
I became more quiet,
Less social, more linked
To Jesus and to the life of prayer.
But He would not accept my simple
And regular litanies.
Now, this demanding Jesus appeared,

> **By your entreaties, You**
> **And your companions shall obtain**
> **My blessings for you and for the world.**

I was to move ahead
With the establishment of a new order
Dedicated to Divine Mercy.
I tried to put off the idea again and again.

> **I want it as soon as possible.**

What should I do?
I prayed to the Virgin Mother,
I cannot separate from my order,
It is dedicated to You after all,

> I am Mother to all,
> Thanks to the mercy of God,
> Do God's will.

What should I do?
Later, she asked me to pray
For the future of my beloved Poland.
One day as I thought over and over again,
I washed the dirt off my hands
And settled into my cell.
There in the midst of the small room
Was a dazzling angel,
An agent of God sent to
Carry out judgments against the wicked.
I begged for mercy for them all—
I argued most of them will do penance,
Then, in the speck of a second,
I was pulled up and beyond

Myself to the glorious throne of God.
Then to Jesus and to the Father
I pleaded for mercy,
And the hand of the angel
Was tightly stayed.
I said a new prayer,
Which was implanted in my heart.

"Eternal Father, I offer You
The Body and Blood,
Soul and Divinity of Your dearly
Beloved Son, Our Lord Jesus Christ,
For our sins and those of the whole world;
For the sake of His sorrowful Passion
Have mercy on us and on the whole world."

I was told to say it when
I entered a chapel and be aware
That it appeases God's wrath.
Recite it for nine days in a novena,
Use the rosary to keep count,
This would be called a chaplet,
Said on the rosaries.

My confessor had that prayer printed up,
And on the other side of the card
Was the image of Divine Mercy.
It was just the beginning
Of spreading the word of Jesus.
This was my message to the whole Church,
To be the Apostle of Mercy.
I tried to write out a rule
For the new community of Divine Mercy.
My confessor found a convent house,
A terrible broken down home,
But Jesus was in the midst of it.

That spring I planted
New crops in Vilnius
To sprout and grow,
But I could not plant
The plan for a new organization.
"What shall I do?'
Jesus had said He wanted
Not just an order,
But a contemplative order,

Just as I had desired when I first
Became a nun and felt so
Disenchanted, so misplaced.
Maybe my vision of Jesus' command
For such a group,
Really was not His will,
But mine being done?
I talked to my confessor,
To my superior, and to the archbishop.
The archbishop felt it would be wrong
To move quickly on this.
"Pray for the world and beg God's mercy,
But as for the congregation,
Wait a while, there is no need to begin.
It is a good idea, but if
It is God's will,
It will be done in His good time."
My confessor felt we had no funds
To support such an effort.
I grew somewhat impatient
With my Lord.
You tell me to move on this,
And then restrain me through
The Church's representatives,
Your delegates.
What do You want?

Almost in response,
I had a vision of six sisters
Receiving communion in a small chapel.
Jesus walked right by me.
"How can You pass me by,
And not say anything?"
He looked over, made the sign of the cross,

**Do not fear anything,
I am always with you.**

I told the Mother Superior
I was leaving the congregation,
But she was patient with me.
She insisted I wait and see what happened.

**Your work is mine,
I am using you as a
Lowly instrument of My will.**

How can I obey my old vows,
And leave to create a new order?

My superior locked me in the tabernacle
With Lord Jesus to see what is His will.
But nothing happened,
Nothing happened in 1936.
My fellow nuns thought
I was being "holier than thou,"
And shunned me.

Then I received from my confessor
The beautiful brochure on Divine Mercy,
With the image and prayer.
It was so wonderful.
But on one Friday,
I had a terrible vision of Our Lady
Who had been so good to me.
Her breast was naked and pierced
And she wept for Poland.
I prayed for guidance,
And Jesus appeared.

> **Say the chaplet over and over.**
> **If even the worst sinner**
> **Says it only once,**
> **He will know My infinite mercy**
> **And boundless goodness.**
> **Trust the world to My mercy.**

I grew ill again,
With pain and paralysis,
How great the sufferings
Of final death must be.

Jesus though came to me:

> **I desire the Feast of Mercy**
> **To be a shelter for all souls.**
> **On that very day after Easter,**
> **I will pour out an ocean of graces**
> **Upon all souls who approach the font**
> **Of My boundless mercy.**
> **Go to confession and communion and**
> **All sins and all punishment will be forgiven.**

The Divine floodgates will be open.

As I grew more ill and irritated,
Sister told me I was not sick,
"They made up the illness, so you could rest."
But St. Michael appeared:

> The Lord hath told me
> To take special care of you.
> I know you are hated by evil,
> But do not fear,
> "Who is like God!"

Still, I feared to tell
My own sisters about my visions,
How am I to tell the world,
And so Jesus seemed to turn away
Because I did not do His will.

Then I had a terrible vision of hell.
It was worse than I or you could imagine.
It was a place of great torture,
A large and extensive sense of nothing.
We feel the loss of God,
The remorse of conscience forever,
The presence of eternal hell,
A fear that permeates but does not destroy,
Continual darkness without a shaft of light,
And a terrible smell—
A stink that will not leave your nostrils.
Can God open up these gates,
Can He let the damned finally go?
I do not know
For God is God,
And we see only the reflections
Of His mind,
Even the mirrors of the damned.
If nothing is eternal,
Can damnation be eternal?
My Jesus knew I could not
Perceive too much of hell,
Too much pain and suffering,
For you see—
I am the Apostle of Mercy.
So many love justice,
Many wish to raise devotion

To a demanding exact standard,
But Jesus chose me for
A different way, a gospel of mercy,
Of love and of redemption.
Any of us can mete out justice for the world,
But it is special to fall back to mercy,
Mercy from His sufferings in the Garden
And then on the Cross.
Mercy is the sister color
Of the purple of the Resurrection.
We can be born again,
Not to judge sin
But to forgive it.
So He says in the gospel of John.

Jesus explained that mercy came
From deed, from word, and from prayer.
Celebrate Divine Mercy, venerate His image,
Speak of His gifts,
But show mercy here on earth.
Faith is of no account
Without good works.
I offer up my pain
For the souls of purgatory,
And can see the souls in heaven
Giving constant praise to God.
Oh, how immense is His greatness,
And He carries me in His arms like a child,
Close to His heart.

As I laid in my hospital bed, I would
Hear the loud noises of the ward near me.
We are such chatterboxes,
Especially the men in the Pradnik clinic.
They talk of everything under the sun,
But of you, My Jesus.
The whole world interests them,
But about their Creator, there is silence.

While there, a girl came to me,
She was suffering much
And was an orphan plunged into pain.
I offered to the Lord my remaining joy
And she was consoled.
At times on the radio,
I heard news of the world,

And of its sufferings.
There was the rise of Germany
And threats to our city of Gdansk.
War was in the wind.
And in my soul,
There was deep discontent.
I am plagued about the congregation:
Still, I have no money, no education,
And am not in good health.
I am in the abyss of misery.

The Lord Jesus saw this

> **I see you are in misery,**
> **But carry out My will,**
> **You are not alone.**

I was sad not to be
Released from that task,
But soon I felt immersed in God,
I began to lose
All sense of what is around me.
I was in ecstasy,
I desire death so much,
I long for You, for the food of love.
Then, He came to me
And told me I was to be His special spouse.
I had already taken my vows,
And was called "the spouse of the Lord."
This was to be a special relationship.

I wrote to the pope asking
To be relieved from my vows,
So as to start a new order;
My superior insisted that
Was a temptation of Satan
To destroy the Divine Mercy mission.
So I quietly prayed to Jesus,
And remembered that
I must perform one act of mercy a day,
I know that it is most difficult
To love those who are unpleasant to you,
I know it in my own life.
I dislike most those who to your face
Are pleasant and happy,
And then in other crowds

Are so critical, so harsh,
For hypocrisy is the greater sin.
One day I sat in the midst
Of a group of nuns, and they talked
Of me as if I were not there.
"She says she is sick."
"She will die, soon."
"She is a saint."
"We will see if that is so!"
I listened like a third person,
Invisible to the sight.

Still I did not know His will.
I felt deserted by God,
Terrible fear pervaded my soul,
Your will be done.
One evening, He reminded me

> **Three o'clock is the Hour of My Passion—**
> **I can refuse no one any request**
> **Of Me in virtue of that Passion.**

Three o'clock was the magic hour.
I must cry out to the whole world,
"Love God, because He is good
And great is His mercy."
Still by day and by night,
I feel the slow disintegration
Of my body even before death.
One nun said it smelled like a corpse
Near her, and indeed it did.

Then in the midst of all of this
Once again I had a bout of ecstasy
Having to do with God.
At times, I just want to live normally,
Quietly, at peace here on earth.

Satan told me—
Think no more about this,
God is not as merciful as you think.
He is a rather vengeful spirit,
Forget those devotions,
Do not pray for souls,
They are simply damned,
By this mercy, you too will be damned.

It looked like my guardian angel at first—
But then I said,
"You are the father of lies!"
And I made the sign of the cross,
And in a rage the figure vanished.

The days passed by
Sometimes I was so sick,
I again could not take the Eucharist.
"Sister, why don't you go to Mass?"
Too good to go?"
What a cup of bitterness I faced.
"You give into weakness too much!"
But even in my worst days,
I wrote down in my diary as He wished:
It was the story of different souls:
The sinful soul, the despairing soul,
The soul striving for perfection, the perfect soul.

At times, seated quietly I crocheted,
And daydreamed of better times:
Of my home with mother and father,
My family, the flowers and the warmth.
It is so nice to walk without shoes
Through the meadow grass, isn't it?

 I have known such despair and disbelief.
Jesus criticized me for
My lack of obedience and lack of humility.
Oh, how will I ever be a saint?
As I wrote in my diary all this,
Satan reappeared—
Banging pots and pans,
Like an old fool in the kitchen.
Mother Superior told me to be quiet at times,
My groans at the terrible pain
Were disturbing other nuns near me.
But I saw Jesus in such pain also,
I am so thirsty,
My lips like my soul are parched.
They never come in here,
Rarely do they stoke the fire,
Or even clean up.
They fear this decomposing body.
So I was alone to myself.
I had much to do,

And one day I noticed in a magazine
That not one saint came from our order.
But Jesus appeared and responded quietly,

> **Do not cry,**
> **You are that saint.**
> **You are My heart.**
> **Speak to the sinner about my Mercy.**

And I knew His ecstasy again.

> **Without you and your intercession**
> **I would send punishments to men.**
> **But you discern My anger.**
> **Say the chaplet.**

I do not fear You
For I know Your Mercy well.
Spread the Divine Mercy devotions,
For there will come a time
After my sorrowful death,
That they will be banned,
My visions denied,
My words suppressed
By the highest authority.
And then Jesus will move
To all that resisted,
And there will spread across the world,
Far beyond Poland
Into new worlds, new congregations,
Small churches and great cathedrals
The gospel of Divine Mercy.

> **You will soon be a saint.**

Out of the depths I cry to you,
Oh Lord, Lord hear my voice.
My Jesus, I will trust in You.
Jezu, Ufam Tobie.

> **I have not come to judge mankind,**
> **But to save it.**
> **Ask for My mercy,**
> **Even the most stained sinner**
> **Can gain salvation.**
> **Tell them, Faustina...**

Tell them…..

FAUSTINA:
Father, teach us how to pray.

JESUS:
Ojcze Nasz, któryś jest w niebiesiech,
święć się Imię Twoje;
przyjdź królestwo Twoje.
Bądź wola twoja,
jako w niebie tak i na ziemi.
Chleba naszego powszedniego daj nam dzisiaj.
I odpuść nam nasze winy,
jako i my odpuszczamy naszym winowajcom.
I nie wódź nas w pokuszenie,
ale nas zbaw ode złego.

Amen.

(Exit, lights out).

ABOUT THE AUTHOR

MICHAEL P. RICCARDS is the author of numerous books and verse plays. His most recent work is a compilation of short stories on his grandfather, *Brief Encounters*, a chronicle of a generous loyal, humble, and somewhat complicated individual. Dr. Riccards has been a college president at three different institutions, a public policy scholar at the College Board, and the founding head of the Hall Institute of Public Policy. He is married with three children and five grandchildren.

Made in the USA
Middletown, DE
30 August 2017